MAKE FLIPPING REAL ESTATE YOUR PART-TIME HUSTLE

BE YOUR OWN BOSS, EARN MORE MONEY & CONTRIBUTE TO YOUR COMMUNITY

Cori Arnold

Copyright © 2020 Corianne M Arnold

All rights reserved.

ISBN-13: 979-8630001948

Printed in the United States of America

CONTENTS

1. **Introduction to Flipping**   7
   My First Flip
   Spend Your Money Where It Counts
   Take Advantage of Free Resources
   Flipping Part-Time vs Full-Time

2. **Flipping vs Other Part-Time Jobs**   20
   Pros
   Cons

3. **Pay for the Property**   40
   Making Personal Finances Decisions
   How to Get Approved for a Mortgage
   Emergency Fund

4. **Structure the Business**   53
   Treat Flipping as a Business
   Sole Proprietor or Partnership
   To Become a Real Estate Agent or Not
   Figure Out Your Flipping Strategy
   Tax Implications of Your Strategy

5. **Find the Flip**   75
   How to Find a Good Flip Property
   Location, Location, Location
   Learn the Permit Requirements of the Area

6. **Purchase the Property**   85
   Don't Over Pay
   Budget Conservatively
   Write the Offer
   Negotiation
   Close the Deal

7. **Execute the Renovation**   114
   How to Contribute Best (Labor v Outsourcing)
   Maximize the Design
   Avoid Rework – do Projects in the Right Order
   Meet the Neighbors
   Quality is Key

8. **Staying Committed**   134
   Power of Focus & Goal-Setting
   Self-Discipline
   Persistence
   80/20 Principle

9. **Sell the Property**   138
   To Stage or Not to Stage
   What to Include When Selling
   Curb Appeal
   How to Determine the Sales Price
   How to Market the Flip Property

10. **Summary of Flipping Rules**   145
    Don't Over Pay for the Property
    Plan, Plan, Plan
    Complete the Flip
    Conclusion

1: Introduction to Flipping

My First Flip

I just signed the documents to purchase my first flip property. In its current form it's not inhabitable. The pink, urine-smelling carpet overwhelms the living room as you enter the house. The kitchen is closed off, dated, and dirty. It has cracked and torn linoleum flooring. On the exterior the wood siding is rotting. The windows are drafty and have metal interior trim. The previous owner rigged a broom handle out of the upstairs window in an attempt to get cable. The garage is a mess, filled with trash and miscellaneous scrap metal. The walls and ceiling are lined with chicken wire, which is holding up half-rotted insulation. There is a tiny bathroom in the basement that is literally two feet wide by two feet deep. The entire bathroom is sitting on a wooden platform. There is a curtain being used as the bathroom door and a very little sink. This area stinks. The basement has a dropped ceiling and wood paneling on the walls. There is no working furnace, and it's February in Ohio.

I'm not sure what I was thinking when I purchased this property, but I knew it was a good deal. I had watched the price come down from eighty thousand dollars to fifty thousand dollars over the previous nine months. I didn't know much about the area, but there was a nearby elementary school, and the street seemed quiet. There were an assortment of ranch style and split-level homes throughout the neighborhood. I was anxious and excited, especially, on the first day I worked at the house. As I turned down my new street, to my surprise there were cop cars parked in the driveway two houses down from mine. I thought – what have I gotten myself into?

I found out later the reason the cops were at my neighbors was because the neighbor behind my property had called due of their barking dog. As I spent more time at the property, I discovered most of my neighbors were older, and the community was quiet and safe.

Before I learned about my neighbors, however, I had a lot of work to get done. I had four months before my lease was up at my apartment. I purchased a small heater and used that until the new furnace and water heater were installed. One of the first things I did was to remove the pink carpet. This house stunk and I wanted to remove any of the potential sources of that stench. The bathroom in the basement was also a stinky source. I demolished that small frame and platform and sealed up the plumbing. All of the floors in the living room and bedrooms were hard wood, but they had been damaged over time. I rented a sander and went to town on all of the floors, that is, after my sister and I pulled up all of the staples and nails. My mom then helped me stain the floors, and my dad helped me seal the floors with polyurethane. This house was definitely a family affair. I didn't have many repair skills back then and needed a lot of guidance.

I also hired a contractor to replace all of the windows and siding. My dad agreed to help on the kitchen remodel. I was actually working at Lowes part-time on the weekends, and my parents removed all of the cabinets for me one day while I was at Lowes. It was great; everything was removed from the kitchen, and we tore down a wall to open up the kitchen to the living room. I was able to get a lot of discounts by working at Lowes. We used stock white cabinets. I had granite installed for the counters. My dad's friend also participated and helped install the new tile floor. Everyone was so generous with their time and skills, and I was learning a lot about renovating a house.

I did most of the painting myself and tried to prepare as much as possible for the days when family were coming to help. By the time June came, I had new windows, but didn't have blinds or any other window coverings. The siding was started but wasn't quite finished. It was June in Ohio, and it was a hot and humid summer. The contractors doing the siding showed up at 6am to avoid some of the heat. That meant, I had to be out of the shower and dressed by 6am unless I wanted to give them a show. This lasted for about a month, and I, then, was finally able to get the blinds installed. I took advantage of another Lowes deal, but had to be patient for the installer to be available.

This project was hard. I was working full-time and part-time, and working on the house to make it livable within the four months when my lease expired. All in all, with the exception of the siding, I was able to make the deadline and get out of the apartment. Although this was a lot of hard work and inconvenience, it paid off when I sold this property for one-hundred and five thousand dollars in 2016. I hadn't purchased this property with the plan of flipping it. I thought I might live here for a lot longer, but it didn't work out that way. With the tax law being very favorable to homeowners who live in their primary residences for more than two years, I was able to walk away from this property with a significant profit and no taxable income. It was awesome collecting that check at the closing.

Throughout 2017 I couldn't stop thinking about the extra income this property made. I wanted to do this again. I started talking to a co-worker about this and found out she had a lot of experience of her own. She had renovated her property when she purchased it back in 2000 and had also renovated her grandmother's property in 2008. She had actually loaned me some tools back in 2012 for my first fixer as I didn't have many tools back then. As we kept talking, we convinced each other to try a partnership to flip properties. At the end of 2017, we purchased our first flip.

Spend Your Money Where It Counts

By reading this book you're likely in the research phase, trying to get as much information in books and through online articles and videos as possible. This is the right research to do. As someone who is becoming increasingly interested in real estate, you are becoming a target for many people who claim to be real estate investors, who want to teach you everything there is to know about real estate. Be careful when being approached by these types. They may know a lot about real estate, but they really just want to sell you information that is likely available online or in books at a much lower cost, or even free.

Don't fall for the charade like this caller I heard on a Dave Ramsey podcast. Her husband was working in a different state than where they lived. He wanted to be closer to his wife, so he took a job closer to their home in the same state, but also had to take a pay cut. In order to try and make up for some of the loss income, they thought flipping houses would be a good option. They decided to go to a seminar, and seventy thousand dollars later they had not yet purchased a property. They had gone seventy thousand dollars in debt from this real estate seminar and had nothing to show for it. The company had told them they were invited to the 'next level' which they were excited about. They were so caught up in the words these individuals were saying that they got off track of their original purpose. When beginning in real estate flipping, there is no information that is worth seventy thousand dollars. The concept of flipping real estate is simple. Find a cheap house in a nice neighborhood that can be renovated and sell it for a profit. Obviously, there is a bit more to it than this, but these details can be learned through the free resources described later in this chapter.

In other seminars individuals try to sell properties in different states in questionable areas. They guarantee they will manage the property for you and vacancy rates are low. The individuals end up getting a commission on the sale of the property to you and 10% of your rent every month. Some of these deals might work out, but if the property is in another state, how will you know it's actually being taken care of? Make sure you do some research on these property managers and on the area in which they are trying to sell you real estate. When you're not familiar with a city, you're not going to know the difference between the 'good' side of the tracks and the 'bad'. You're trusting these property managers to make a good decision with your money. Be very careful.

In other seminars they try to sell oddly shaped parcels of land that they say are worth a ton, but in reality, these small pieces of land are really never going to appreciate significantly. They are usually not big enough to build a property on, and generally, they are in random spots. One of my friends had built a property, and there happened to be one of these small parcels right beside her property, which was owned by an out-of-state individual. This piece of property basically was a triangle at the corner of the street neighboring my friend's property. My friend wanted to purchase the parcel, but the owner wanted a ridiculous amount for this small piece of land in rural Ohio. She never purchased it, because she knew the owner wouldn't be able to build there and was never around. You don't want to get yourself stuck owning these random parcels which you cannot liquidate or utilize.

Take Advantage of Free Resources

There are so many ways to get information for free or low cost these days. The Internet and technology have helped to create an abundance of information on almost every topic imaginable. Maybe you do not know the ins and outs of the permitting requirements in your area. This is why you can either personally reach out to your municipality or hire a contractor who will. Maybe you have also never picked up a hammer or a paint brush. This is why you research and hire a contractor. There is so much free information on the Internet that you can find and can easily become proficient in the world of real estate. Maybe this won't get you the best contacts, but it will give you an understanding of the process and work that goes into flipping houses. Before spending a lot of your hard-earned money on seminars, try out the following free resources to learn about potential flip properties or get advice on the ins and outs of flipping.

Real Estate Agents

There are a lot of steps when it comes to purchasing real estate, but this is why you have a real estate agent. Your real estate agent knows the market, knows what type of properties sell the quickest in your area, and can even give you tips on what she would change to get the biggest bang for your buck. Their job is to answer all of these questions. Real estate agents almost always have a network of other agents, investors, and clients. Interview multiple agents to get an understanding of their network and their knowledge of the local market. Choose the one that seems to have the most knowledge. As you continue to use this same agent, she will likely find you more deals. With the networks these agents have, you may have an abundant pipeline of potential flip properties if you find the right agent.

To find the agent that's best for you, you can search using various methods. One way is going to the Zillow website and clicking on "Agent Finder". From here you can enter your zip code, or if you know an agent, you can type their name in directly. This allows you to see reviews of the agent as well as recent sales and listings. Another way to find agents is literally to visit agency offices and interview them firsthand. Ask them questions, such as the following:

1. How long have they been in real estate?
2. How many transactions do they average per year?
3. What areas are their main focus and do they venture into other markets?
4. Do they prefer to work with buyers or sellers, or both?
5. Are they familiar with any properties right now that might be good flipping candidates?

6. Do they have any clients currently that flip properties?
7. What types of properties sell best in their market? (size, price, features)
8. Do they work with real estate investors often?

By asking these questions, you will get a sense of whether this is a person you want to work with or this is a person you never want to meet again. You may meet someone who is in her first year of real estate, but has a strong focus on clients who are flippers. This might be a better agent for you than someone who has been in the business for twenty years.

Property Managers

Property managers make money by managing rentals on behalf of the investors who own those properties. Property managers are therefore in the center of the network of investors wanting to buy and sell properties. They are always looking for more investors to expand their business. Even if you are not a potential customer because you want to flip and sell versus flip and rent, they will still most likely talk to you and provide insight to deals they know about. They may give you a condition that they represent you as your buyer's agent meaning they would get an agent commission when you purchase the property, or they may ask for a referral fee for telling you about the property. Never pay a property manager upfront. They can be very beneficial since they have relationships with many investors, but make them do the work of getting you a property at a discounted price before paying them any referral fees.

Open Houses

Another great free resource is open houses. My business partner, Deb, and I wanted to branch out into a new city for our third flip property. We didn't know any real estate agents in the area nor did we know the area that well. One Sunday we decided to attend as many open houses as we could. The benefits of attending open houses include seeing the neighborhoods, comparing other flip properties, and meeting real estate agents. By driving around to different open houses, we got a first-hand view of the streets, the curb-appeal of the houses, and the feeling in each of the neighborhoods. These are all important considerations when finding the right flip property. You want to find a neighborhood that feels comfortable to be in and seems welcoming.

The second major benefit of attending open houses is you get to see other flippers' work. We were stunned to see the poor quality of some of these houses. In one house the flipper installed laminate flooring, but they didn't put quarter-round molding between the laminate flooring and the existing baseboards. In other words, there was a gap between the flooring and the baseboard trim. It looked horrible. In another flip property, the person had replaced the flooring with new carpet. It seemed nice. However, the flipper didn't do anything with the kitchen. The new carpet made the house feel clean and refreshed, but walking into the kitchen felt like walking into a different home. There was one cabinet for the sink and one other cabinet. There wasn't a place to store anything. This was an older home, and there was only one tiny bathroom on the first floor. The two bedrooms were upstairs. It would have been much more convenient for the buyers if there was a bathroom upstairs. I'm not sure how difficult it would have been, but adding a bathroom to the upstairs seemed like the right thing to do. Seeing the quality of this work was shocking. I can't believe there were buyers willing to purchase these homes in this condition. Learning this was great. We knew our work was superior to these.

The next benefit to attending open houses is meeting real estate agents. As I mentioned earlier, real estate agents are an excellent resource when it comes to finding your next flip property. After we had exchanged business cards with them, a few of them followed up with us, sending us listings they thought might be good flip property candidates. Real estate agents are one of the best resources you can have as a flipper. Be transparent with them though if you are already working exclusively with another agent. You don't want to lead someone on thinking they might get a commission when you have no plans of ever using their services. They still have incentive to meet you as they may list your next flip property. They would still get the commission from representing the seller of the flip property. As long as you are clear upfront what information you're looking for, they will be a great asset moving forward.

Real Estate Groups

When I moved to Los Angeles, I found a real estate group that hosted a few events each month. These were free events to attend. Most of the events hosted a company or individual who was looking to sell property or services. I was tempted to purchase a few of these services, but in the end didn't think this was for me. The great thing, however, was that I learned a lot just by attending these events. I convinced my boss to attend one of the events with me, and she learned about some VA foreclosure properties that were for sale at a significant discount. Even though she didn't end up using the property managers that were hosting the event, she was able to purchase quite a few properties in 2008-2009 when the market was at the bottom, rent those properties, and now, a decade later, has cashed out a couple of them at double what she originally paid.

If you can find a real estate group near your city who hosts free events, you only have your time to lose. Why not attend and see if there is anything you can learn. Don't get swept up by the sales pitches though. Keep your long-term goals in the back of your head. If the sales pitch sounds too good to be true, it probably is. You will at least have a few more contacts for potential future deals. Try searching for these types of groups on LinkedIn, Facebook, or Google. There are also real estate groups in certain colleges too. I know UCLA had a group that I could have joined while I was going to school there.

Realtor & Zillow Apps

Technology has improved our lives in many ways. In the past the MLS (multiple listing service) database was only accessible to real estate agents and brokers. With the increasing technology, however, two companies have been able to share much of the information that is in the MLS database: Realtor and Zillow. These are two apps where you can search properties for sale in your area and filter down into the specific features you are looking for. The filter criteria aren't quite as creative and detailed as the search criteria within MLS database, but these are still two very helpful resources for looking at available properties. They are completely free. You'll just need to sign up for an account, and you can search unlimited. I'm on these apps almost every day looking at new properties for sale or using the data to come up with comparable values.

Other Flippers

The best advice you can get is from other flippers. Although some might consider you competition, most flippers are happy to give advice and tips they've learned from their experiences. See other flippers as mentors or peers in which you can trade information. For example, they may have insights in certain areas that would help you avoid buying in the wrong location. They may have relationships with vendors or retailers that might be able to extend their discounts on materials to you. Tracking down flippers can be difficult, but you can find them at sheriff sale auctions, via real estate agents, and by driving down the street. Foreclosure auctions tend to attract a lot of different types of people, including the lenders who have the lien on the property, the former owners, neighbors, and flippers who are looking for a good deal. You may ask your real estate agent if she works with any flippers who are open to allowing you to contact them. Another good way is literally to watch for houses that appear to be under renovation as you drive by them. In many cases these renovations are being done by flippers. Not everyone will want to give you information, but many will be generous with their guidance. These local flippers know the specifics of your area.

For example, what price range is the best flipping range? We've found in rural Ohio that the mid-one-hundred-thousand-dollar range is hot. It's high enough to warrant some nice updates, but low enough to allow younger buyers to be able to afford it. This price range wouldn't work in major metro areas though. You may not even be able to find a distressed house for one-hundred thousand in the major metros. Find out the average home price in your area and stick to that range.

What areas are in most demand in your city? Moving to the new city for our third flip was a risk. Neither of us knew the area very well. One of our co-workers visited the property in our first month there. She had grown up in this city and informed us that we had bought on the wrong side of 12th street. We were right on the edge of what the locals considered the bad side of town. It worried us at first, but we started meeting the neighbors on both sides of the house, and realized that our flip was nestled right between to families who prioritized taking care of their homes. What features do buyers expect to be renovated in your area? Some areas have buyers with specific expectations. For example, stucco exterior is popular in the southwest United States, but wood or vinyl siding is common in the mid-West. Local flippers will know the answers to all of these questions and more. If they've been in the business for a while, they will have houses that sold within a day and houses that sat on the market. Ask them what patterns they have experienced in selling their flip properties. You may learn enough from their experiences that you will avoid buying a loss-generating property.

There are no shortcuts to making money in real estate. Take the time to do some research or ask an agent or another flipper which areas are selling well, where the good deals are, and what are the best areas of improvement for the biggest bang for your buck. Be patient when saving up the funds to purchase your first property, and be patient when you find your first potential flip property. Patience gets you good deals. If you're in a hurry, you will finance the property and pay too much because you want it too badly, and you will have your blinders on to other options. What I mean is that you'll get too excited when negotiating with the seller and will concede your position, giving them a premium price when it's not necessary or beneficial to you. Stand your ground and wait for a good deal. There are a lot of properties out there.

Flipping Part-Time vs Full-Time

I know you're excited about getting into real estate. Buying my first flip property was exciting. I couldn't wait to start tearing up carpet and improving the house. Remember, you've gotten where you are today because of your full-time income. This is the income that has allowed you to have a consistent paycheck, pay for your lifestyle, and save for retirement. You make a specific salary that you can likely depend on in the months and years ahead. Before quitting this stable full-time job to embark on your new flipping career, try flipping part-time first.

Even if you have extra funds saved, it's not smart to quit and jump into flipping full-time. Flipping is hard work and takes a lot of commitment. What if you start your first property and hate it? By starting slowly, flipping your first property part-time while continuing to work full-time, you can see if flipping is something you really enjoy. You won't have the same pressure when flipping part-time versus full-time. There are so many variables in flipping a house that quitting your steady income job may put you in a bad place financially. For example, let's say your first flip goes as planned. You found the property quickly, improved it, and sold it for a profit. But, looking for your second property, you find that the market is different; the potential flip properties aren't going for the same discount you saw last year. It may take you six months to find your next flip property. Will you have enough savings to cover this dry spell of six months plus the time it takes to improve the next property and get it on the market and sold?

Dave Ramsey says frequently to callers, "don't jump off the boat until it's close enough to the dock." When he says this, he is referring to someone's full-time income compared to their part-time income. In other words, don't quit your full-time job until your part-time income is close enough to the full-time income to easily be enough to live on. Depending on how quickly you plan to renovate the properties, you may only do two or three properties a year flipping full-time. If you can make twenty-five thousand dollars per property and complete three properties, seventy-five thousand dollars is not a bad annual income. Not all flips make twenty-five thousand dollars though. There are risks, including not finding the properties quickly enough, not getting a good enough deal on the purchase prices, and unexpected expenses that come up during the renovations. If you have never flipped a property before, you should be conservative on the number of houses you expect to flip per year and the profit expectation per each flipped property.

Once you've executed a few flips, you will know if this is the right career for you. To be honest, after three flips I am still debating if I want to go full-time or keep this as my side hustle. For me right now, it will continue to be my side hustle. It's an awesome side hustle. It gives me the flexibility I need, and I enjoy being part of the improvement of a property and a neighborhood. I love the hands-on approach to it and the tangible results of the renovation.

Flipping real estate is one of the best part-time hustles available. I haven't flipped a hundred properties or made a million dollars flipping, but I have flipped three properties over the past four years and made around sixty-eight thousand dollars profit in addition to working a full-time job. This isn't a get rich quick book, but it is a book that will give you the knowledge to get rich in the long run. If you made an extra twenty-five thousand dollars each year, which you could invest, you'd have improved financial security after just a few years. This is a book for the person who is interested in real estate, who doesn't mind getting dirty doing demo, and who wants to make extra money on the side. If you have patience, can commit to a project, and like to learn new things, flipping real estate is the side hustle for you.

2: Flipping vs Other Part-Time Jobs

You might be in a situation where you are contemplating working a part-time hustle to earn extra income to pay off debt, to increase your monthly investing, or to challenge yourself. Whatever reason you've decided to start looking into part-time hustles, consider flipping real estate. There are many options when considering the right part-time hustle. You could work retail on the weekends, teach part-time college classes, work in seasonal industries, be a real estate agent, work labor in the evenings, deliver pizza, design websites, etc. The list could go on and on. There really are an infinite number of part-time hustles available. You can choose to work for an employer or work for yourself. I've always wanted to have my own business, but never knew which product or service to sell. I wanted to find something that suited my interests and something that would allow me to contribute to a higher cause. For me, flipping is that avenue. Through flipping, I have been able to meet a wide range of individuals, have improved neighborhoods, and have sold a good product to the buyers. Below are just a handful of the pros and cons of flipping property.

a. PROS

Flexibility of Being Your Own Boss

My full-time job is volatile. I work in finance. We have really busy weeks, and we have a few down days during every month. Most of the time this volatility follows a pattern, but I can't always predict when the busy spells will happen. I can't count on finishing work every day at 5pm in order to fulfill a part-time evening schedule. If I wanted to give up every weekend, I could commit to that, but even then, I sometimes travel for my full-time job on Sundays and occasionally on Saturdays. With my unpredictable full-time schedule, I can't and do not want to commit to a part-time schedule of an employer. I want some flexibility and ownership of my own hours.

In flipping you choose how fast you want to go and how many hours you spend each week at your flip property. You are in charge of this project and its timeline. The hours you work are very flexible. If you want to start at noon on Saturday or 6am on Sunday, that works. Your flip property is open and available whenever you are willing to be there. The only exception to this flexibility is potentially using loud tools too late at night or too early in the morning. Other than disturbing your neighbors, you have 100% flexibility for when you want to work. At many part-time jobs, you are on a schedule, and most employers do not offer this flexibility. In addition to this flexibility, you can also change your mind quickly. For example, if you have plans one evening that get cancelled at the last minute, you can visit the flip property and put in a few hours that weren't expected. Many part-time employers would not allow you to change your mind at the last minute like this.

You can also choose your scope of work. Which work do you want to do, and which work do you want to hire out? At a part-time job you are going to do the jobs your supervisor requests of you, whether you like them or not. At the flip property, you can decide if you want to paint or hire it out. You can decide if you want to install new kitchen cabinets or have them hired out. You can base this decision on your own time capacity and budget, but the decision is ultimately up to you. Although Deb, and I do much of the work ourselves, there are parts we dislike. One of those is mudding and sanding after the drywall installation. Although we haven't outsourced this yet, it will be one of the first jobs we outsource on our next flipper. In addition, Deb is a great electrician while I don't want to touch it. She spends a lot of time on the electric while I spend more time on framing and painting. We have the flexibility and competence to work on separate projects, which we each prefer.

The downside of all this flexibility is if you don't have discipline, you may not work often enough to complete the house in a reasonable timeframe. For example, if you sit on a property for too long, the overhead (property taxes, insurance, utilities) will start eating into your profit margins. To avoid this give yourself weekly and monthly goals of either hours spent or projects completed at the flip property. Projects completed might make more sense. If you end up spending a lot of hours at the property but do not accomplish much, this won't get you to the finish line of selling the property.

In addition, if you do not set a timeline or intermediate goals, you may end up completing the property in the cold winter months. Real estate sales tend to slow down dramatically in the winter. You would not want to complete a property in December or January and put in on the market then. There won't be as much demand as in the summer. It's best to put flip properties on the market in the spring or summer when there is more demand.

Contribution to the Community

You've driven past those houses that bring down the whole block, right? What if you had the opportunity to clean up that house and help the neighborhood shine? Flipping done correctly revitalizes neighborhoods and helps communities. This is a huge part of why I like flipping properties. Think of some of the neighborhood projects you've been involved in. Many volunteer days are spent planting flowers or cleaning up playgrounds. These projects give life back to these areas and invite people to utilize the playgrounds for what they were meant for, play. In the same fashion, we are improving an entire property. This includes a huge boost to not only the inside of the property, but especially the curb appeal of the property.

We didn't realize when we purchased the second flip property, which I'll refer to as the Ditmore property going forward, that we were buying the 'druggie house' on the block. This is how many of the neighbors referred to the Ditmore house. It was a disaster. There was trash everywhere. We thought we were just making the street look better, but we were actually helping all of the neighbors. We started talking to the neighbors on the left, and they said they were ready to move because of the constant partying and safety concern they felt. They were aware of the hiding places drugs were stored in the front yard and had witnessed people picking them up. They had seen others walk through their back yard to get to this house. They were an older couple and felt vulnerable to this situation. We talked to the neighbor on the right, and he said he had to put blankets and heavy material over his windows to block out the noise every night. We had no idea what these neighbors had been experiencing before we purchased this property.

One of the first things we did when we bought the Ditmore house was to call the local police to have them come and impound an old Dodge truck sitting in the driveway. On a late December evening the police arrived and hauled it away. We watched from the inside the house, excited to have a cleared driveway. We were slowly but surely ridding this property of all the trash that had consumed it. We then found out a few weeks later that all of the neighbors were also cheering in their living rooms when that truck was finally moved. Everyone was excited to see that old pile of rust leave the neighborhood. We later discovered it had been sitting there for years.

The third flip property, which I'll refer to as the Meadow property, was an estate sale. The prior owner's wife had died about ten years prior to the husband dying. After she passed away, he stopped taking care of himself and the property. He was so saddened by the loss of his wife that he kept her tin of ashes on a living room chair for the rest of his life. The neighbors told us this story about the ashes as well as stories about getting his groceries for him. They could barely stand the smell of him when they dropped them off. When we first got into the house, the bathtub wouldn't drain. I doubt he was taking many baths. He hadn't done any maintenance to the house or yard in many years. Vines were growing through the fences. The decks were rotting away. The siding had years of mold growing on it. A good power washing and the addition of new decks on both the front and back significantly improved the curb appeal. As we were working on the front steps, we actually had drivers giving us thumbs-up and yelling, 'good job' out their windows. It was really satisfying knowing we were doing something good for the neighborhood.

In addition to the neighborhood improvement we invited the sister of the wife who had passed a few years earlier back to the Meadow property for the open house. She seemed horrified in how her brother-in-law had treated the place. During the original closing, she had given us photos of how the house looked when her sister was alive. It was a cute bungalow decades ago. When she saw our finished product, she was in tears saying she wished her sister could have seen the house now. This moment was the most satisfying part of flipping this property. Properties deserve to be maintained and to shine. They can have a real impact on individuals and communities.

Tangible Results

Flipping is a very hands-on and tangible process. At the end of a long day, seeing the change from how an area looked in the morning compared to what you achieved that day is a satisfying feeling. Some days are long and tiring. Demo is fun, but it is laborious and can be dangerous. Seeing a wall down or a room painted is a tangible change that you can not only see, but feel. Bringing a property back to life after it has been trashed for years does something to you. I can't describe how it feels other than satisfaction and fulfillment. It is a stressful part-time hustle, but there are a lot of rewards that come with it. It's giving purpose to a vacant and neglected house.

The Meadow property had layers and layers of cosmetic changes which were old and outdated. It felt like we kept pealing layers away, from the carpet on the floors to the dropped ceilings to the pine paneled and plastered walls. The previous owners had added dropped ceilings, which made the ceilings two feet shorter, making the rooms feel smaller. We ripped out all of the dropped ceilings, giving the two front rooms a grand, spacious feeling. They had also added pine paneling, which we could have left up, but we didn't. We generally go all in and gut the interior of the houses we flip. This means that for most of the first few months, we may very likely make the house look worse than when we originally bought it. This happened to us at the Meadow property. When we removed the drop ceilings, we damaged the plaster on the walls and created significant holes in the ceilings where the frame of the drop ceiling was attached. When we removed the plaster and lathe from a few of the rooms, we created a lot of dirt and holes in the walls. For us the demo phase lasts for at least a month, and it's generally three or four months before the house starts to look any better. It's easy to get frustrated in this first phase of the flip as the goal, of course, is to improve the property, not make it worse. However, once you pass the demo phase, the rebuilding and cosmetic updates start to improve the look as well as start to motivate you to keep going.

Whether you are doing the labor yourself or hiring it out, flipping is a very tangible job. You are changing how a house looks and functions. In my full-time job there are parts of it that are tangible and hands-on, but it's nothing like the experience of improving a property and seeing the expressions on people's faces when they see the final product.

Stay in Shape

This may sound odd, but if you decide to do most of the labor yourself and you choose some physical projects, there is a very good chance you will lose some weight and a few inches. During the Meadow flip, I did not run on the treadmill or do any other workouts the entire nine months of the project. I was stronger by the end, and my jeans were loose. The demo phase of this project was significant, removing the plaster, a wall, the dropped ceilings, the pine panels, the cabinets, the counters, the bathroom fixtures, and the carpet. This equates to a lot of lifting and carrying of these items to the trailer to be hauled away. Removing all of these items takes strength. The previous installers installed these using strong nails, staples, and glue, making the removal a bit more difficult than normal.

If you're ready for a physical part-time job, doing most of the labor yourself might be the answer. Demo is especially good. If you are taking multiple trips to the dumpster, you can count all of that walking as cardio. I am part of a Fitbit group that has challenges almost every weekend. During the demo and framing weekends, I would almost certainly win the steps challenges. This made the rest of the group mad, but they were able to beat me during the weekends I painted as painting doesn't seem to accumulate too many steps.

On the other hand, I was very sore after a few projects. For example, installing the new laminate flooring took a lot of up-and-down movement, cutting the pieces and laying them. I could barely walk multiple days after the flooring was installed in both the Ditmore and Meadow properties. The other downside is that you are likely not going to get a consistent workout. Some muscles were used every time I worked at the property, and some did not get used at all. In order to avoid letting some parts of your body get weak while others get stronger, it's probably best to continue your normal workouts during the flip. There aren't too many part-time jobs where you can say you actually get in better shape throughout the job. This was an added and unexpected benefit.

Ability to Make More Money

Because you are your own boss in flipping, you can make much more in flipping a property than many part-time jobs. On the Ditmore flip, we made roughly forty dollars per hour. On the Meadow flip, we made roughly twenty-three dollars per hour. I didn't keep track of my hours on the first flip, but as you can see the rate was nearly cut in half between the second and third flips. As we continue to work on differently aged homes in different neighborhoods, we are understanding which houses make for good flipping candidates and which do not. In a normal part-time job, you are given your rate upfront, and it generally stays flat. The good thing about this is you are guaranteed this rate. The bad thing is this rate is likely low. There are some part-time jobs that are commission based as well. These tend to pay higher rates, but you don't get paid unless you successfully sell your service or product.

This is why I love flipping properties; the profit potential is outstanding. Get a good deal on the right property in the right neighborhood with a good market, and you'll make a nice profit. As you embark on this journey, you will become better at not only finding the right properties, but also budgeting more accurately and understanding which projects bring in the best returns. The more you research and learn about flipping, the better position you'll be in to make higher margins. If you follow the tips from this book, you will be miles ahead of your competition and will have a higher probability of making more money.

Learn New Skills

Although I had a background of helping my dad, who is a handyman and seems to know everything there is to know about remodeling projects, I really didn't know much when it came to renovation. For example, on the first flip property, which I'll refer to as the Elm property, my dad and his friend came over and installed most of the tile for the kitchen floor. I helped put the mortar onto the tiles, but dad laid them and his friend cut them. Now, two flips later, I am confident in my ability to lay tile, to space it correctly, and to install the backer board, which is the layer that is installed prior to the tile being installed.

I also didn't have much experience framing, but in the Meadow flip, I framed in the new wall for the bathroom, and framed in the space for the two new showers. We moved a couple other walls to extend the size of closets and closed up doorways, and I knew exactly how to plan them and build them. These are projects I never thought I'd be able to do on my own, but now I have a lot more confidence.

I have always loved learning. I thought my learning would come from my full-time career, but it's very rewarding to learn other skills that may never complement my full-time career. Understanding how to remove a toilet and install a new toilet is something I never thought I would learn, but it's a good thing to know. My understanding of how the mechanics of a house work gives me a lot of confidence in my own primary residence. Learning gives me a bigger perspective, and these are practical skills that I can use just about anywhere. Even if you determine flipping isn't the part-time hustle for you, you can use these skills and knowledge while working construction, being a real estate agent or property manager, or even just owning a home. If you know the mechanics behind a project, even if you don't do it yourself, you'll understand the appropriate cost and time it will take to complete the project, as well as possible obstacles that present themselves as the project begins.

b. CONS

It's a Big Commitment

I know I just said a lot of good things about flipping properties, but don't make this decision lightly. Most part-time jobs will allow you to work for a month and quit. If you do this, it generally doesn't cost you anything other than your potential future income from the job. The company would still pay you for all of the hours you worked during that first month. If you get half way through a flip project and decide you hate it or you can't afford it, you won't be able to sell the property for a premium when the work is only partially completed. You may see your progress and think you've added value to the property, but many buyers don't want to start projects that have already been partially started. Some of the best deals on properties are when a previous flipper has tried to flip a property but either ran out of funds or patience. These half-demoed houses or even half-renovated houses will sell for a discount. You don't want to be the seller in this scenario. If you sign up for a flip property, make sure you see it through to the end, or it will cost you big time. In all three of the flips we've done, there was a point early on in the process where we had invested time, labor, and a little money, but the properties were in worse condition than when we had purchased them. For example, if we had paid fifty thousand dollars and now the demo is done, walls and ceilings are torn down, it is very unlikely that we would be able to sell the property for fifty thousand dollars. Maybe we could get forty thousand dollars if we find the right buyer, but we'd have real estate agent and closing costs on top of the loss in the purchase price, plus the loss of all of the time we had invested.

Commitment to see this project through to the end is a critical consideration when you dive into the world of flipping. No one wants to be worse off after putting their hard-earned sweat and time into a project. Before committing to the purchase of a property, create a plan and budget. If you know exactly what projects you are planning to tackle and understand the approximate cost of those projects, you'll be in a better position than someone who just jumps into flipping without thinking through the process. Planning correctly is half the battle when it comes to flipping. Having a plan allows you to have short periods of frustration without calling it quits, because you know exactly what projects you are under-taking and can visualize the finish line. When you do not have a plan, there is no set finish line, and therefore it's hard to see the light at the end of the tunnel. In flipping, things always get tough. Even with a plan, you're going to come across unexpected issues, whether that is physical issues with the property or communication issues with vendors and contractors. By having a plan, even a basic plan, which shows your high-level budget, timeline, and projects, you're much more likely to see this project through.

Risk of Losing Money

Unlike most part-time jobs, there is a risk of losing money in flipping. You need to be fully aware of this and understand whether you can handle losing money on your flip. No one ever wants to lose money, especially not on something you are devoting your time and energy to, but it is possible. I never thought I would lose money on a property, but I made a mistake of purchasing a duplex when I was younger in the wrong area and sold it for ten thousand dollars less than I had paid for it four years earlier. I didn't do the right preparation and research on that property, and paid for this mistake in the end. If you decide to enter the world of flipping, know that this is a possibility. Even though I lost ten thousand dollars on that duplex, that mistake made me more cautious when beginning to flip. In fact, looking back, I'm happy I made that mistake when I did, because the loss didn't kill me, and for the lessons I learned, it was great experience, showing me what I liked and disliked about real estate.

You can definitely decrease the chance of losing money by following the guidance in this book. Make sure you are getting a deal on the property you purchase by looking at the values of the neighboring and comparable properties. For example, if you are planning to pay more than ninety percent of the neighbor's value for a similar house that needs a lot of work, you're not going to make money. If your potential flip property is for sale for ninety thousand dollars, and the comparable properties in better condition are worth one-hundred thousand dollars, you're only going to be able to sell your flip in the range of one-hundred thousand dollars. After closing costs and costs of improving the property, there will be a loss. Generally, you'll want to purchase the property for less than fifty percent of the sales price you are planning to sell the property for. For example, on our three flips, we paid, on average, 47% of our total sales price. There are other variables to this, especially the scope of work you are planning to undertake at the property, but this rule has worked for us. Other flippers refer to a 70% rule, which basically says your purchase price of the property plus the renovation costs should not exceed seventy percent of the planned sales price or ARV (after repair value). We have stuck closely to this 70% rule as well.

Another way to lose money is to not budget accurately. We'll look at budgeting in more detail later, but the budget you create when discovering a potential flip property can make or break your profit in the end. We are very conservative in our budgets to avoid the risk of losing money. So far, we haven't lost money on a flip. We do add a hefty contingency to our budgets, because things come up frequently. For example, in the Meadow property we didn't expect to purchase a new furnace, but one day, the old furnace just died. We could have had the bad part replaced for nine hundred dollars, but the furnace was so old that many companies wouldn't service this furnace any longer, and another part could have gone out after this one was replaced. We decided to upgrade to an entirely new furnace, which was around four thousand dollars that wasn't in the budget. Because we had been conservative on the budget in regards to what we paid for the property and what we thought we could eventually sell it for, we still made a profit, just slightly lower than what we expected.

At the Ditmore property, we didn't expect to spend much money on the driveway. However, the existing driveway was only about eight feet wide. We could barely fit two vehicles back to back on it. We decided to have the old pavement torn out and replaced with gravel. This was a twenty-five hundred dollar hit that wasn't planned. It made sense though. No one wants a single-lane driveway where someone always has to park behind the other person. It's an inconvenience that we were able to solve, and ultimately, it helped us sell the property faster.

There can be many expensive items that come up unexpectedly.

The furnace, water heater, and air conditioner are likely the most common. Roofs are expensive. If you find a flip candidate, make sure the inspector checks out the roof. This isn't an item you want to pay for, and if you need to pay for it, ensure it's included in the budget. Other expensive items that can come up unexpectedly are replacing an outdoor storage shed, garage doors, windows, and siding. You may walk through the property once and purchase it without taking enough time to look at the condition of the garage doors, for example. Always keep a buffer or contingency in your budget.

Potential Physical Injury

You may not have considered this, but doing the work yourself can be dangerous. Our families have participated in the flipping projects, especially during the demolition phase. My sister joined us one Saturday morning and was assigned the job to demo the back porch. She was ripping off this paneling-like material from the walls and ceiling. Suddenly, she came in with a board attached to her hand. She had put a nail through her thumb while pulling this material off of the walls. She wasn't able to pull out the nail with her other hand. I'm usually a real wimp when it comes to blood, but for some reason when this happened, I was able to hold her hand and pull out the nail. She was fine in the end. I think she was more disappointed that she couldn't help more that day.

On another day Deb's niece was there. We were using a saw to remove the kitchen cabinets and countertops. We made the mistake of not looking inside these cabinets. As she was sawing through the counter and cabinets, we all saw a spark. She had cut right through a live wire. Luckily, she didn't get shocked or injured, but that could have easily happened. We are usually very safety conscious, but in this case, no one thought to check inside the cabinets for wires.

There were other injuries at each of the flip properties, but none have been life-threatening. We've been very lucky. We always try to use the proper safety equipment as well. We use masks for much of the project. We actually invested in the heavy-duty masks that have changeable filters for us and our families. There is a significant amount of dust created when removing plaster and lathe. Also, if you are painting or doing any work with strong fumes, disposable masks and air ventilation are key. Safety glasses, knee pads, and gloves are among the other items we have invested in.

No one wants to ruin their long-term health over a part-time hustle. Make sure you take the right precautions when doing these projects. If you're not doing the work yourself, ensure your contractors have their own insurance and make sure your home owners policy would cover any accidents on the site. Having all of these checks in place will not only give you peace of mind, but will protect you in case anything does go wrong.

Cash Flow not Continuous

At many part-time jobs you receive a bi-weekly or monthly paycheck. It may not be the same amount every pay period, but it is usually consistent from one paycheck to the next. Flipping properties has a very different cash flow phasing. There is a large outflow at the beginning, assuming you're paying cash or putting down cash up front. There are more outflows as the work begins. The cash collection doesn't happen until the very end of the process when you have sold the property and the sale is final. See the chart below.

The darker line represents the consistent paychecks over the year. This represents a standard part-time pay from an employer paying you fairly consistent checks over the course of a year. You never have to worry about payday, because you know you're getting paid. You don't need to worry about when your paycheck will arrive because your employer sticks to a schedule. If you've shown up for your assigned hours or delivered all of the work you were given, you can expect a paycheck. You can also see with this darker line that it never goes below zero. You will likely never need to pay an employer to hire you; you should only receive paychecks, keeping you cash-positive the entire time you're employed.

The lighter and more volatile line is the cash flow from flipping property. You will either pay one-hundred percent cash or pay a large down payment. In either case, there is a significant amount of cash coming out of your pockets at the beginning of the flip as represented by the downward line in January and February. As you renovate throughout the year, you will pay for materials and labor. Especially toward the end of the flip, when you are adding bathroom fixtures, lights, kitchen cabinets, counters, and appliances, your cash will get consumed quickly.

You can see how important having a planned budget and timeline is. These tools will give you some idea of when you can get your money back, determine your target date for completion, and establish your target date for listing the property on the market. The only control you have over how quickly your flip property sells is the price you have it listed at; you can't control the market. Expect the worse from a timing perspective. In other words, assume it will take longer to sell than the average property on the market. Selling it anytime sooner than your expectation would be a favorable situation.

This chart makes it clear that you will need to have back-up cash to fill the timing gap between when you purchase the property and when you sell it. This is why continuing to work your full-time job is important, especially when you just start flipping. By having your stable full-time income, a budget and a timeline, you'll be able to plan ahead and have enough funds to cover this dry period.

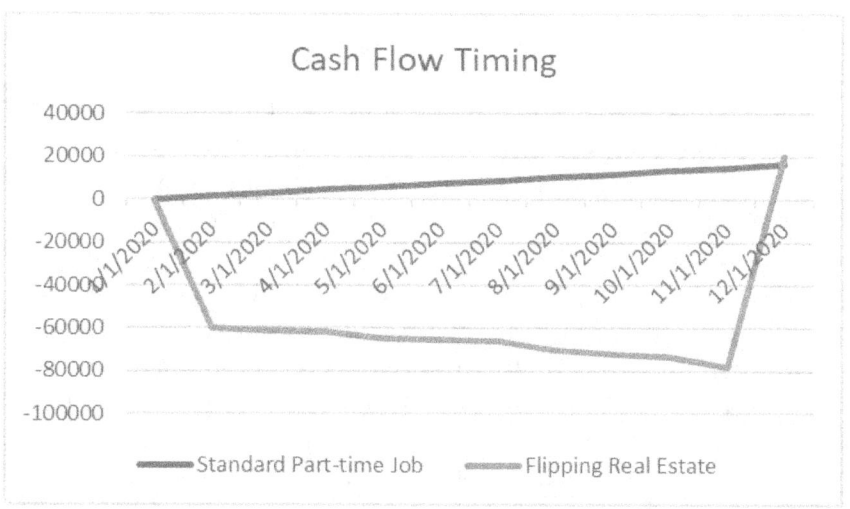

Higher Stress Level

Because there is more risk built into the property, and the cash flow comes at the very end of the process, flipping real estate seems to be more stressful. At almost every stage of the work, there are unforeseen items that come up; the furnace dies, the electric is worse than expected, the property floods, or the property has termites. These are all things that can happen, and there are many more issues that may be discovered as the work progresses and walls are opened up. You, as the flipper, are responsible for all of this. In addition to discovering these issues throughout the process, you don't control the real estate market. It may be a seller's market when you start the flip, but by the end, you're in a buyer's market, where there are too many sellers and not enough buyers. In this type of market, the price premium you expected when you purchased the property may be smaller and therefore your net profit would take a hit.

When you work at other part-time jobs, you are accountable for providing quality work, but you aren't generally responsible for any losses incurred while you are working for an employer. If you happen to drop a pizza or drop some merchandise while stocking a retail store, most of the time, your employer will take the hit for your mistake. But, in flipping, any mistake you make is on you. It comes out of your net profit in the end.

Owning too many properties can become burdensome and stressful in itself. Vacant properties tend to attract robbers and squatters more than your primary residence. We have been lucky in that we've had watchdog neighbors at all three properties. The neighbors actually ended up calling the cops on us at both the Ditmore and Meadow properties. At the Ditmore property, I left Deb at the property to do some work while I ran to Lowe's to get some more materials. I returned to find a cop car in the drive way. One of the neighbors saw movement in our property, and hadn't seen my vehicle. They thought she was an intruder. Deb was a little startled and offended, but we were both happy the neighbors called the cops with suspicion.

At the Meadow property, Deb was there by herself again. We had just purchased the property and had only been there a couple times previously. The neighbors didn't recognize her vehicle and called the cops. In both cases we were surprised and actually relieved that they were ready to call when they had suspicion. It was great to know that we had watchdogs on both properties.

At most part-time jobs, you get paid by the hour. While flipping real estate, there is a point where your profit starts decreasing by the day. The longer you take renovating and selling a property, the more overhead expenses you will incur which add no value to the property. Overhead cost examples are property taxes, insurance, interest, and utilities. The longer you spend on a property, the more overhead or non-value costs you will incur. The opposite is true for a many standard part-time jobs. The more hours you work, the more money you earn.

While flipping can be more stressful, it can also be more exciting and more engaging. I don't want to emphasize the stress too much, because this stress can lead to higher profits if the market turns your way. In the Ditmore and Meadow properties, we ended up selling both properties over list price and over our expectations. Even though issues come up a lot during a renovation, those issues can drive you to improve in other areas of the budget or require you to be more creative in other areas. Stress isn't always a bad thing as it will move you out of your comfort zone and allow you to grow.

Time Required is Significant

You are most likely working full-time and have many commitments. How much time are you really willing to devote to your flip property? Flipping a property is a commitment. It's not 'hire a contractor' and the house is done. Even if you decide to hire out 100% of the work, you still need to spend time at the property making sure your contractor is implementing the agreed upon updates. Because time management is critical, we started tracking our hours at the flip properties. Deb and I both each spent around four-hundred hours at the Ditmore property. If we had worked on this full-time, we could have been done in ten forty-hour weeks, or two and a half months. However, we had full-time jobs. These four-hundred hours came from weekends and evenings. We purchased this property in January 2018 and sold it in September 2018. It took eight months to renovate it and a month to close the sale of it. We worked some weekday evenings, but the majority of these hours were weekend hours. If I average these out, we each worked about twelve-to-thirteen hours per weekend. If we include the time we spent at our full-time jobs, we each worked about fifty-five to sixty hours per week. Make sure you're willing to put in the hours before purchasing your first flip property.

The purchase of the Meadow property closed in December 2018, and we closed its sale in November 2019. We spent almost every weekend of 2019 at this property. Because this was an older house, and we almost did a complete gut job, we each worked about five-hundred hours at this property. Renovation takes time and commitment, especially if this is your part-time hustle. The upside is that no one is mandating that you finish within a specific time period. If you want to only work at the property one day a week, that's up to you. That's the best part of this part-time hustle.

No one is dictating how fast you progress other than yourself and potentially your significant other. If you do have a family, your commitment may cause resistance as you are taking time away from them. You'll need to balance this project with all of your other commitments and responsibilities. If you and your spouse decide you both want to do this together, that helps tremendously as you can work as a team and figure out together how much time you want to devote to this.

To finish the Meadow property before winter came, we ended up working about twenty-four days straight at the property. That included weekends and evenings during the week. This property was forty minutes from my home. Driving there every evening for these twenty-four days was burdensome and exhausting. But knowing if we waited until November to get this property on the market, we might miss our chance at a quick sell. In Ohio, the colder it gets, the slower the market gets. Generally, buyers want to be settled in their new home before the school year starts. We had aimed at finishing the property in August or September, but it took these twenty-four days in September and October to get it on the market by the beginning of October. This timing still worked out great as we ended up being in contract within twenty-four hours of putting it on the market. And, we were able to sell it above the asking price.

Understanding the market ebbs and flows and being able to work many days in a row might be required for you to get the best price for the property and the quickest sale. If you are willing to set aside these evenings temporarily to get the best return on your project, flipping is right for you. If you can't see yourself giving up a few evenings after work, flipping might not be your best part-time hustle.

Another factor is the distance between your primary residence and the flip property. The Ditmore property was located in the same city in which I worked. It was easy to run over there after work and spend a couple hours. The property was about thirty minutes from my primary residence though. On the weekends, I was spending an hour each day driving. Because it was located in the same city I worked in, it didn't seem too bad. However, the Meadow property was located forty minutes from my primary residence and also about forty minutes from my work location. Every day that I worked at this property, I was giving up an hour and a half of driving time. If I worked during the week, I generally wouldn't get to the flipper until around 5:30pm which didn't leave much time for actual work on the property. Consider the distance between your primary residence and your flip property as the more minutes you are commuting, the fewer minutes you are spending on the renovations. This is not only a loss of time, but also more costs in gas and mileage on your vehicle.

Overall, how much time you devote each week is one-hundred percent up to you. The upside of only working at the property once a week is that you have more time for other commitments. The downside, however, is that overhead costs, such as utilities, property taxes, insurance, and potentially trash and mortgage interest will be higher. Every additional month your project gets delayed is more money going towards these overhead items and less profit for you at the end of the project.

3: Pay for the Property

Making Personal Finance Decisions

One of the first things you'll need to figure out is how are you going to pay for this property? If you're looking for a part-time hustle in order to get out of debt, then you likely don't have five or six figures just sitting around in your bank accounts. If you do not have any extra funds saved up, I would recommend putting flipping on the back-burner until you are able to save up some money. It's going to be really difficult to get approved for a loan if you do not have any money to put down. Instead of jumping into flipping, consider coming up with a plan to save over the next year or two until you're financially ready to jump into a property.

During the Ditmore flip, Deb and I each put in forty thousand dollars to purchase the property and do the improvements. We paid fifty-eight thousand dollars for the property, leaving us around twenty-two thousand dollars for the renovation. We ended up exceeding that twenty-two thousand dollars, and each needed to deposit another four thousand dollars about eight months into the project, partially to cover the extra costs and partially to give us a cushion in case any additional surprises came up. You'll need to have extra cash in case your contingency doesn't cover all of the issues you discover during the renovation. If you don't have extra cash available, you may find yourself needing to borrow more money just to finish the renovation.

Or, if you're not able to borrow, then you may need to sell the property before all of the improvements are complete. Selling a property that is partially demoed and partially improved won't sell at a premium. You may need to even discount the sales price in order to sell it. This would likely result in an overall loss. This is not a situation anyone ever wants to be in. Ensure you've got the funds to complete a project before you sign the offer. If this means waiting longer to start your flipping business, wait. It's much better to be patient than to rush into it and risk losing money.

Emotional Impact of Cash vs Debt

I know you're excited and want to purchase your first flip property, but patience really is a virtue. I was very impulsive in the past and jumped into commitments without thinking them through all the way. For example, I was so excited to be a landlord that I purchased the duplex without much saved or much thought. I did some research about being a landlord and having the right documents, but didn't take the time to research the property like I should have. Getting too excited about a deal makes you jump faster into something. You take on risks that don't have to be risks. Had I done more research on the duplex I would have offered a lower price to the seller, and my purchase price ceiling would have been much lower. I made these dumb decisions because I was using debt to finance this property, and by using debt, I inadvertently took more risk than I should have. If you start using cash for all of your purchases, including personal purchases, you will think more about each purchase. Had I used my own cash to purchase the duplex, I would have done all of the research I needed to do, and would have entered that negotiation with the seller with much more insightful knowledge.

When I purchased the duplex, I didn't have any experience buying real estate, and I didn't follow any rules. I also made the executive decision that my parents, who had never managed property, would be my local property managers as I was in Los Angeles. My parents didn't volunteer for this. They didn't have the experience or desire to do this. Four years later we had evicted multiple tenants, and those tenants had done some serious damage to the property. And, I ended up with one of the former tenant's dog, Lady, who I still have to this day. All in all, I roughly broke even from a rent to mortgage payment perspective, but what I failed on was the purchase of the property. I paid a premium price for a duplex in a non-premium location and in a non-premium condition. I was so excited about the purchase and the dream of owning real estate that I didn't follow any guidance that might hinder my ambition to buy this property. I sold the property in four years after I had purchased it for ten thousand dollars less than my original purchased price. Fortunately, this error happened early, and this loss didn't kill me. It was worth the experience and education.

What did I learn? Don't let yourself get emotionally attached to a piece of property, and the money is always made at the buy. Staying emotionally unattached is very difficult when you are starting out. Owning property, especially for the first time, is so exciting. I'm going to have my own piece of land in this country. As sellers negotiate with you, the bidding back and forth can get heated. It can easily become a competition, where your competitive emotions start to surface. You get into the state of winning at all costs the ownership of the property instead of sitting back and understanding that if this property doesn't work out, there are thirty more in this area. There isn't a shortage of properties in most areas. There is a house on almost every corner. Remember that there are plenty of houses available for you and don't get caught up on one specific property just because you want to 'win' the property. If you end up paying too much for the property, you haven't won anything. The profit is made at the buy. In other words, the profit is made when you purchase the property at a price lower than market value. Make sure you say this a few times to yourself before adventuring into your first deal.

For the Ditmore and Meadow properties, we used 100% cash to pay for each of these. By using our own cash, we take a more conservative approach when choosing the right property. It does take longer to find a property at a price we will accept, but we have also always made money. Cash slows our decision-making down, but it increases how much we research each and every property. When you are buying with your own cash, you feel the weight of your decisions. When you buy with the bank's money, you don't feel the same weight, and based on this lower burden you make more rash decisions and spend more money. I finally became debt-free in 2016 and since then, I have been making much better spending decisions. How do you become in a position to pay all cash for a flip property?

Budgeting

Budgeting your personal spending is the answer. Do you know how much your total debt is right now? If not, list out all of your credit card and loan balances and monthly payments. If you total those columns, you'll see your total debt and your total monthly payments. Before you undertake any flips, you should strive to get your consumer debt (all debt except your mortgage) paid off. I know in most cases, that might take years. It took me years to pay off my debt. Think about your long-term goals. Would you rather continue going out to eat or would you rather flip a property? In order to pay down your debt, you need a plan. This plan is the budget. Create a budget for yourself that eliminates much of the excess spending you do each month. I know you enjoy going out to eat and your extra media subscriptions, but these are only short-term sacrifices. Include in your budget how much debt you can pay off each month. Any excess dollars should be paid to the debt you are focusing on. There are a couple ways to pay off your debt. You can start with the highest interest rate debt first or you can list your debts smallest to largest and pay off your debt in that order.

Benefits of paying the higher interest rate loans first are evidently the savings in interest expense. This is how I paid off my debt because I had some large, high-interest student loans. For me this method worked and allowed me to be creative in finding ways to cut my interest expense. One of those creative ways was using zero-interest credit cards. Being organized and paying these off on time meant no interest for around twelve months, which ended up saving me a lot of money. I also cut as many other expenses as possible out of my life. Being persistent in these two areas really catapulted my debt reduction and eventual savings growth.

Another method to tackling your debt is Dave Ramsey's debt snowball. He advises to start with your smallest debts and pay those off first. With these quick results, the momentum of paying off the small debts will grow as you pay off the larger debts. Either method works if you are committed to getting out of debt and willing to sacrifice your life style. This sacrifice doesn't have to be a permanent change. It's temporary while you are getting out of debt. When I was getting out of debt, for example, I had received a free Keurig machine, but realized I was spending $10 a week on the K-cups. This wasn't a necessity, so I got rid of the Keurig machine and saved $10 a week. This might sound like small savings, but an extra $40 a month towards debt can make a mark over time.

Look at your auto-withdraws on your bank account. Are you still using those subscriptions or memberships? Can you live without them for a couple years while you focus on getting out of debt and saving for your first flipper property? These short-term sacrifices will make significant long-term goals a reality. Buying your flip properties will allow you to make overall better decisions and will slow you down. You don't want to rush into your first property. Remember, don't get emotionally attached and always be able to walk away from a deal. Not every deal is one you want to do. Working with your hard-earned and saved cash will slow you down and let you make better decisions for the long-run.

Cons of Leveraging

Another popular ploy by these real estate seminars is convincing you that leverage, created by debt, is a great tool to use to purchase real estate. The more leveraged you are, the more properties you can buy. And, the more properties you have, the more profits you can collect, right? That might be true in theory, but leverage adds significant risk. The more leveraged you are (or the more debt you have), the more risk you have. For example, if you own one property that was paid for in cash, and your tenant stops paying you, you can evict him. You don't have to rush to find another tenant; you can take your time and find a good tenant. However, if you have eight properties, all with mortgages on them, you are dependent on the tenants' rent in order to make your monthly payments. What if all eight tenants decided to stop paying? You would have to come up with eight mortgage payments. You may have to come up with these payments for multiple months while you evict these tenants. Then, because you are dependent on these rents, you will need to rush to get the next tenant into the property. You may not do the same level of background screening because you need the rent money. This starts a vicious cycle of not being able to make the mortgage payments and leasing to bad tenants, which could ultimately lead to foreclosure or bankruptcy. These seminars do not talk about this perspective though; they only describe the upside of leverage.

While in Los Angeles, I joined a real estate group. They offered classes and events where we could meet property managers. I really enjoyed going to these events. The hosts were almost always there to sell you something, but at the same time, I could always learn something too. And, these events were always free. They even provided food at most of these events. You know they wanted you there to sell you something. But, luckily at the time I didn't have a lot of extra funds, so I kept attending and learning as much as I could. The founder of this real estate network talked about how he had accumulated over 100 properties. He talked about purchasing one, and then stripping that first one of all its equity by refinancing it to buy the second property. And, this was the cycle. Every time the properties appreciated, he would go to the bank and refinance the property, take out the cash, and use that as a down payment on the next property. He also admitted that he had declared bankruptcy due to this method.

In addition to this founder going bankrupt, Dave Ramsey also admits that when he was in his twenties, he bought into this idea of leveraging in order to continue buying properties. I believe Dave was flipping properties when this happened to him. His bank was purchased by a larger bank, and that bank called all of Dave's mortgage notes. He wasn't able to sell the properties quickly enough and ended up losing everything he had worked toward and filed bankruptcy.

No one wants to go through a foreclosure or a bankruptcy. You are getting into real estate to make extra money, not to lose everything you have. If you can pay cash for a flipper property, that is the ideal situation. You will avoid all of the loan fees by paying cash. I can't imagine how much in fees the founder from above paid over his lifetime of refinancing every time he wanted to cash out equity. If you don't have the cash today to pay for a property, at least wait until you have 20% down. With 20% down on the property, you will avoid paying the extremely high interest and the PMI (property mortgage insurance). You will still pay a higher interest rate than if you were purchasing a primary residence. The banks also see flipping property as a higher risk and therefore charge the customer for taking the higher risk on the flip property.

In summary, make sure before you sign up for any real estate seminars that you create boundaries before attending the seminar. Don't go in without any boundaries and let your emotions get sold products and services that don't take you to your end-goal of flipping properties.

How to Get Approved for a Mortgage

Although leverage is not the answer to building an empire of flipping properties and rentals, I do understand that you may not have 100% cash to pay for your first flip. Even though I really do recommend waiting until you've saved up all of that cash, if you want to jump into flipping sooner with a mortgage, here is some information on types of lenders and how to get approved.

Local Banks vs Mortgage Brokers vs Hard Money Lenders

There are different lending options when finding the right lender for flipping. Because you are not planning to reside in the flip property, the lender will see this as a higher risk than if this was going to be your primary residence. This higher perceived risk means the interest rate will be higher. Your local bank or credit union is likely the least expensive option. They will generally charge the lowest rates and the lowest closing costs. However, it may be the most difficult to get approved through your local bank. They usually only have a handful of products they offer, and if the flip loan doesn't conform to their standards, they won't be able to loan you the money. In many cases, they might be willing to use a hybrid, where you receive the funds to purchase the property and then they release the renovation funds as you make progress on the renovation. You will most likely still need to come up with at least the 20% down. On the Elm property, I, luckily, had a good relationship with my local lender. She approved me to borrow the funds for the purchase of the property, and then I was given an additional fifteen thousand as the renovation was being done. I believe I was only approved because I had planned to live in this property, which I did for the next four years. My relationship with the lender was likely the primary reason I was approved. She told me she was sticking her neck out to get me this loan. I really appreciated that and definitely paid it on time every month, and eventually paid it off when I sold the property. Because I was planning to live in this property, I also didn't get hit with the higher interest rate or higher closing costs. If you know a local lender, you will get the least expensive products through them. These loan terms will also likely have the normal mortgage term, fifteen to thirty years.

Mortgage Brokers come in all shapes and sizes. During my

lending days, I became familiar with many of the programs they offered. Theses lenders are much more expensive than local banks. An example of a product they offered was the borrower needed to put down 25% cash, and the mortgage broker would provide the funds for the purchase price and then the progressive payments for the renovation, up to the 75% mark. The interest rates they quoted were between 8-10%, when other mortgage rates were between 3-4%. They also had outrageous closing costs. Remember, every dollar you spend on interest and closing fees is a dollar less in your pocket when the flip is complete. If you're flip property doesn't net a significant profit, you may be giving all of your profit to the mortgage broker. The upside to mortgage brokers is that you will have a better chance of getting approved for the loan. Some mortgage brokers specialize in flipping loan products. They understand the higher risk and make you pay for it, but on the other hand, they may be your answer to getting approved.

With both local banks and mortgage brokers, you will be required to start making payments when the property is purchased. Depending on how they set this up, you may likely be paying principle and interest on the total loan value even though you haven't pulled all of the renovation funds yet. These payments may incentivize you to get the flip finished quickly, as this is additional cash flow out of your pocket each month.

The final category of lenders are the hard money lenders. These are the most expensive category of lenders. If you can't get approved via your local bank or a mortgage broker, you may want to research some hard money lenders. These lenders will weigh the value of the collateral much higher than your credit score. They assume that they will get the collateral if you can't pay. They want to ensure that collateral value will cover their outstanding loan value. These lenders generally only loan funds if you can provide 30-50% cash down. The terms on these loans usually last between one-to-five years, meaning you either need to refinance or sell the flip property within that time period. The payments you pay are usually only interest payments on the loan value. This means if your flip project takes two years and you've only been paying interest payments, you will still owe the full value of the loan two years later. Paying only the interest may help ease your cash outflow during the renovation, but these loans are very expensive. They literally may eat away your profit plus more. I wanted to give you some information about these lenders, but I would never recommend this type of financing. Given all of the other types of overhead costs, such as utilities, insurance, property taxes, if you add these lending costs, it's almost impossible to make a decent profit. Why put yourself through all of the headaches and labor of a flip project if you aren't going to make any money?

Four C's of Lending

In order to gain approval from the local banks and mortgage brokers, you're going to need to prove that you are a low-risk customer and will pay back the bank all of their money. To be approved, you need to think like lenders. Put yourself in their shoes. They are looking for the lowest risk customers in which to offer their products. Lenders don't want to lose money just like you don't want to lose money. Prove to a local lender or mortgage broker that you're a good bet, and they will bet on you.

How do you become one of these preferred, low-risk customers? You must demonstrate that you are a trustworthy and reliable person that will pay back your debts. The more confident lenders are in your willingness to pay them back, the better chance you have at being offered the best rates. You demonstrate this by scoring well on the 4 C's of Lending, which are Credit, Collateral, Character, and Capacity.

Credit is how you score with the three credit agencies: Experian, TransUnion, and Equifax. These three companies track your payment history, collections, and bankruptcies. Your credit report provides a lot of information about you and how well you pay your debts. Lenders can usually find patterns in credit history that indicate how likely it is you will pay them back. Your credit score is the most critical item a lender looks at when deciding whether you will be approved or not. If you do not have a good credit score, here are some tips that can boost your score.

Start making every single payment on time. Every time you are thirty-days late making a payment, this dings your score. Don't make anymore late payments. Late payments not only hurt your score, but they also incur late fees. Late fees are just additional funds coming out of your pocket. You need to hold onto as much money as you can if you're going to be a professional flipper. Another thing you can do to increase your score is pay down on the credit cards that are close to being maxed out. The ratio of your balances to your total credit is a very influential score indicator. For example, let's say you have three credit cards, each with a five thousand-dollar credit limit, meaning you have a total credit limit of fifteen thousand dollars. The optimal total balance on those cards should be less than 33% or five thousand dollars. If you have a higher balance, your score will suffer. If you have more than 90% of your cards credit limits outstanding, then your score will suffer immensely. Get those card balances paid down. Focus on these two actions, making payments on time and paying down balances, and your score will increase substantially.

Capacity is the next most important area, and tells the lender how much cushion you have between your monthly income and your monthly debt payments. This ratio is called the debt-to-income ratio and can tell a lot about how people manage their money. When applying for a loan, you will be required to provide proof of income, either through a pay slip or through tax returns. In most cases, you must provide at least two years of tax returns and W-2's or 1099's. If you are a 1099 wage earner, this generally means you are a contractor or earn your income via commissions. Because commissioned income is usually less consistent than W-2 income, you must provide two full years of 1099 income. The lender will also pull your credit report as mentioned above. In addition to showing the score, the credit report tells the lender how much you pay in monthly debt payments, giving them enough information to calculate how much capacity you have to make an additional mortgage loan payment.

In addition to the debt-to-income ratio, the down payment that you are able to bring to the table is an important piece to capacity. Can you prove to the lender that you are capable of saving up a down payment and showing them that the funds have been in your checking or savings account for at least a few months? When flipping, you'll almost always need to come up with 20% cash down in order to be approved.

Collateral is another important C and can take the form of many items, including vehicles, real estate, shares of a company, or anything that the lender deems valuable. In this case the property you plan to flip is the collateral. The flip property is the asset the bank holds a lien on in exchange for giving you the loan. A lien is a right of ownership the bank can use if you breach the loan contract in any way. For example, if you purchase a flip property, the lender will hold a mortgage on your property. This mortgage gives the right to the lender to foreclose on your property if you do not abide by all of the terms in the note.

Character indicates how consistent or reliable you are and what kind of relationship you have with that specific lender. How long have you been at your current job? How long have you been at your current residence? Do you have a loan at this lender already in which you have perfect payment history? Lenders care only about a few critical factors when establishing your character for a loan application, therefore you must ace these. Having a prior relationship with this lender is the best way to get approved. When you have a relationship, that lender knows you and your values. She knows, even if this flip goes south, you will find a way to repay the loan. When you have this type of relationship with a lender, you can almost always count on getting approved.

These are the 4 C's of lending. The lender simply wants to know that you're a good investment. From their point of view, they want to know how likely it is that they will get their money back if they loan it to you. As a caveat all lenders weigh these 4 C's according to their own internal policies as well as potentially look at other factors. These just happened to be the 4 C's at the bank where I worked.

Emergency Fund

Hopefully, either with 100% cash or a combination of cash and debt, you will have the ability to pay for your first flip property. This is one of the first steps to starting your flipping journey. The more money you can save up prior to the purchase, the better. You'll always want to have extra funds in case the project costs more or the property doesn't sell as fast you expected. These reserves should be large enough to cover any issues that arise during the execution of the flip. There is not a set value this emergency fund should be, but in my experience if you have at least 10% of the purchase price plus three months of your personal expenses sitting in a savings account, you should be safe.

Because you are continuing to work your full-time job, you'll continue to have cash flow from these paychecks which should also help if issues do arise at the flip property which require more funds.

4: Structure the Business

Treat Flipping as a Business

If you decide flipping is the part-time hustle for you, treat it like a business. Keep costs as low as possible, track all of your expenses, and open a separate checking account.

LLC vs DBA

Since I planned to live in the Elm property, I didn't have to do anything special and didn't do anything formal. I paid for all of the renovations from my personal checking account. I kept track of the expenses and kept receipts just in case I decided to move out before the two-year timeframe. When deciding to make the flip property your primary residence, you will not even need to complete a schedule C on your taxes. You are merely improving a personal asset. When you sell the property, your title company will ask you if you lived in the property as your primary residence for at least two years and if you ever rented out the property. If the answer is yes to the first question and no to renting, they will complete a form which exempts this profit from your income taxes. This tax loophole will be described in more detail later.

For the Ditmore flip, we decided to make this a bit more formal. We opened a personal checking account in our names, and put the house in our personal names. When we got ready to sell the flip property, knowing we were going to make a decent profit, we finally opened the formal LLC (limited liability company). We needed something more formal for our tax returns that year. If I had done the flip myself, there is a strong possibility that I would not have opened the LLC, but instead, would have recognized this profit on a schedule C with the DBA (doing business as) company name. If you are an individual pursuing flipping by yourself or with your spouse, you can report using the schedule C on your taxes and avoid the LLC fees. If you are partnering with anyone other than your spouse, the LLC is the best way to go.

The LLC allows you to have multiple partners. You and your partners agree on how the ownership interest is split. For example, in our business articles, we have defined that each of us own 50% of our LLC, because we have each put in 50% of the cash, and both of us do the same amount of work on the property. You may have a different percentage split, and one partner may put up more cash while the other puts in more labor. If you decide to do an LLC, ensure that your bank account is in the LLC name and that the property is purchased under the LLC name. Keep all of your personal funds separate from the LLC account. For example, don't use your LLC checking for personal expenses, and don't use your personal checking for flip expenses. As you need funds in the LLC account, transfer them and recognize the change on your LLC financial statements.

LLC's are beneficial in that if for any reason you are sued, the plaintiff can only get the assets in the LLC, meaning that your liability is limited to the cash in your LLC checking account and any properties or assets under the LLC. If you are worried about your personal assets, then go ahead and open an LLC. Again, make sure you keep your LLC funds and your personal funds separated. If you don't, this is called comingling, and the LLC can be sued for your personal assets. Our insurance guy told us a story about a friend of his who was comingling funds between his business account and his personal account. He was actually sued, and the court went after him personally because he had been comingling.

How do LLC's work on taxes? LLC's themselves do not pay any taxes on their profit. The LLC is a pass-thru which passes on the profits to the personal income taxes of the owners. For example, if our LLC made ten thousand dollars last year and I am a 50% owner, then I would show five thousand dollars additional income on my tax return. Deb would show five thousand dollars additional income on her tax return. We each receive a form called a K-1 form, which shows each owner's taxable income. You can find more tax information regarding LLC's on the IRS website (irs.gov) or by talking to your tax professional.

ROI (Return on Investment)

In treating flipping as a business, you will be less inclined to make decisions with your emotions, clouding your judgment on the right investments. All decisions, when buying or renovating, need to be made with the thought of return on your money. For example, when you find the right flip property, you will compare the future estimated sales price of the property against the purchase price of the property plus the renovation costs. If the future estimated sales price is two-hundred thousand dollars, and the property needs fifty thousand dollars of work, then you would use these two variables to determine your purchase price ceiling. Let's say the potential flip property is listed at one-hundred and ten thousand dollars. If you paid this price plus added the fifty thousand dollars of work, your total cost in the property is one-hundred and sixty thousand. When you sell it for two-hundred thousand, you'll need to subtract twelve thousand for real estate commission cost at 6% and four thousand for miscellaneous closing cost, leaving you with twenty-four thousand profit or a 12% return (see equation below). You can almost make 12% by investing in mutual funds without any hassle, hard labor, or time at the flip property. Therefore, you'll need to expect a higher return in order to buy this property. The maximum I would pay is ninety-four thousand, which would equate to a 20% return. We target 20% on all of our properties, but because there are always unexpected issues that come up, we usually end up around the 17-19% range.

(ARV – ARV*6% Real Estate Commissions – $4,000 – Purchase Price Ceiling – Renovation Cost) / ARV => 20%

($200,000 – $200,000*.06 – $4,000 – $110,000 – $50,000) / $200,000 = 12%

($200,000 – $200,000*.06 – $4,000 – $94,000 – $50,000) / $200,000 = 20%

You will face this same decision-making strategy during the renovation phase of the flip. For example, are you going to spend $6 per square foot on flooring or will you spend closer to $2? It very much depends on the market you are in, the overall price of the property, and what buyers expect in that area. If you can spend $2 per square foot and your buyers will be happy, then do it. If you are in a higher-priced area where specific types of flooring are expected, then you may need to spend the $6 per square foot to get the right return on your investment. Every dollar you put into the property needs to be justified by a higher ARV (After Repair Value). When making these decisions, however, don't go too cheap as they may drive buyers away. They want to see quality work and quality materials in their home. Weigh the return and the demand of the property together to avoid spending too much or too little on the materials you choose.

Never price yourself out of an area. If the most expensive properties in your area sell for two-hundred thousand dollars, then don't put two-hundred thousand dollars into the flip property. You will never get the return or make a profit. Don't expect the market to rise just because you over-improved one property. Use the information you are getting from your local market to understand the most appropriate price you can sell your flip property at and work your renovation budget from this. To find this data, request it from your real estate agent, who can use the MLS database to search recent sales prices. The MLS is likely the most efficient way to search and filter this data. You are flipping properties to make a profit and to make a return on your money. Remember this as you are looking for properties and creating budgets. Your goal should be to maximize your return and maximize the satisfaction of the buyer at the same time. There are going to be trade-offs on both sides, but what improvements get you the best return while also giving the buyer the most satisfaction?

Cash vs Debt

Another way to make better decisions is to use cash for everything. Dave Ramsey says this a lot on his podcast. We make better decisions when we are making purchases with cash. This is true. I feel different, less risk-taking when I'm making a big decision with my own money. For some psychological reason, when I borrowed money in the past for my side hustles, I was always less risk averse than I am today. I was using borrowed money and taking higher risks. It felt natural to almost gamble with this borrowed money. But today, I use my own cash for all of my side hustles. I do make different decisions. I analyze everything a lot more than I used to. It takes us a lot longer to find the right flip property because we analyze it, look at comparable properties, and estimate the budget. This is why we likely haven't won a property at an auction. We are pretty conservative, thinking the worse might happen in all of the properties we bid on. We may not win as many properties as we could have, but we haven't lost money on a flip yet.

We save everywhere we can. If you have the cash to pay for the property, do it. You will save on lender fees and interest. If you can't put down 100%, then most lenders will lend to you at the 20% to 30% down payment minimum since this is a non-owner-occupied property. Because the property is not your primary residence, the lender will charge a higher interest rate. There is more risk associated with someone who isn't depending on this property for shelter, and you can more easily walk away from this property than your primary residence. The lender knows this and wants to protect themselves from the higher risk by charging more fees and interest. If you can wait another year when you have saved up enough cash to purchase the property for all cash, then all of these lender fees and interest can be avoided. Maybe you look into a cheaper area instead and then slowly work up to the price range you'd prefer to be in. Anywhere you can cut costs, do it. There will be renovation costs that add up quickly.

Limit Overhead Costs

Another set of expenses that do not represent any actual improvement to the property are what I refer to as overhead: property taxes, insurance, trash, water, electricity, gas, mortgage interest, and HOA fees. Determine roughly how long you believe you're going to be working on this property. From the point you close the purchase to the point you close on the sale of this property you will be required to make monthly payments for all of these items. Even though these are all required, none of them improve the value of the property. Therefore, the longer you own the property, the higher all of these expenses will be. For example, sitting on the property for two years versus one year would double all of these costs. Are there any that can be avoided? You can decide to take all of the trash to your personal residence and avoid additional trash fees. You might purposefully avoid properties in HOA's. Another example of a potential fee is the maintenance of the yard. If it's summer time, you may need to either have the yard mowed every week or mow it yourself. These are all things that need to be included in your budget.

Insurance

Since this is a business, you may consider insurance. We always purchase property insurance for the flip properties. This is a given as you never know what can happen on your property. We did get a quote for a business insurance policy, which would cover our tools and some other assets, but the cost didn't seem worth it. We ended up not getting the additional insurance. Insurance is another cost. You want to minimize your costs where you can within reason. If you feel strongly though that you need additional insurance, do it. It will give you peace of mind and allow you to focus on the flip progress instead of worrying about it.

Sole Proprietor or Partnership

Another consideration is working with a partner or not. Being a sole proprietor can be motivating. You own your own business. It lives and dies based on your contribution. You will not have to split the profits with anyone, but you will also need to put in 100% of the cash. As a sole proprietor you are your own boss; you make all of the decisions. You are not dependent on anyone else.

If you decide to go in on a property with someone else, you will essentially become each other's bosses. Communication, agreement, and compromise will be vital to making a partnership work. Deb and I complement each other well. She is always looking for ways to save money and find a bargain while I like to indulge in certain items for the flip properties. It has worked out so far. We end up spending in some areas and finding bargains for other areas. Another way we complement each other is our skill set. She is a great electrician and plumber. I am better at framing and painting. We both work on the design together to come up with the best layout and use of the space. We do argue a lot throughout the process though. There are many small issues and decisions that need to be made in the moment. We may not agree on every small issue, but we find a way to move forward. If she wins one battle, then I am likely to win the next. There are many decisions where neither her or I feel that strongly about, and therefore one of us makes the decision and moves on.

Trust is Key

Make sure your business partner is someone you trust and know well. In order to work as a partnership, you will open a bank account and each deposit funds. Once these funds are in the account, your partner can easily withdraw all of those funds and leave the country. There is nothing you can do about it, because her name is on the account. Trust is a key to this partnership working. I would never decide to partner with someone I just met as there is too much financial vulnerability at risk. If you have a trustworthy sibling, relative, or spouse that has an interest in flipping, that might be the person for you.

There are a lot of benefits to having a business partner. If you do not have enough cash to come up with the 20% down payment, you could each come up with 10% instead. Or, maybe having a partner would allow you to pay 100% cash for the property and avoid financing altogether. This means you only need to come up with 50% of the purchase price plus 50% of the renovation costs. Or, maybe you provide more labor to the project and your partner provides more cash. How you agree to split the ownership must be in writing. If you are doing a partnership, it may be beneficial to open an LLC in order to make the split official and to help make your tax process more transparent.

It is also good to have someone to bounce ideas off of. There are many ways to improve a property, and two minds are better than one when maximizing the improvements that bring in the highest sales price. Having two different perspectives on the future buyer gives you a better vision for the updated features that will have the biggest bang for your buck.

Lastly, it's nice to have someone else who is working towards the same goal. When I purchased my first fixer upper, the Elm property, I purchased the property myself. Although my family was a huge help, there were many evenings where I was there by myself working. Working by yourself with your own vision can be empowering, but it can also be lonely and overwhelming. There were a lot of projects in the first property. I had the goal to make the property my primary residence which helped to motivate me, but some of the projects were so tedious and time-consuming that I wasn't sure I ever wanted to do this type of project again. Having someone else who has 'skin in the game' makes you feel like you are part of a team. People can make other people perform at a higher level than they would by themselves.

An experience that reminds me of this was the orientation for my MBA program. We did a ropes course with different tests. Our first challenge was individual. Each of us had to climb a telephone pole and stand on top of it, then jump towards a trapeze bar. Of course, we were harnessed to safety ropes in case we fell off the pole. I don't like heights, and standing on top of a telephone pole thirty feet in the air scared me, but I was able to do it. A guy in my group, however, was more afraid of heights than me and couldn't stand on top of the pole. In the next event we had to partner with someone in our group, and guess who I was partnered with? I was afraid he wasn't going to be able to do the next challenge based on how that telephone pole challenge went. The next challenge had us each on a rope standing and facing each other, and leaning on each other with our hands to keep our balance. We then had to walk across, roughly twenty feet, hand by hand, step by step. This challenge seemed more difficult because we were higher in the air than in the first challenge, but somehow this guy who couldn't stand on the telephone pole was able to get higher in the air with me, and we successfully crossed the twenty feet. This experience taught me how people can step up more for other people than when they are trying to accomplish something on their own. It really surprised me and made an impact on me.

I believe this is true in flipping when working with the right partner. We can do more together than individually. But, again, your partner needs to be someone you can trust. The last benefit to having a partnership is that if you decide to do a lot of the work yourself, you'll have someone at the property to do the work with. Projects go much faster when there are two people working on them versus one. For example, we tiled the bathroom floors in the most recent flip. My partner used the saw while I laid the tile. It went really fast with the two of us. If I had tried to jump up and cut each piece before laying the tiles, the job would have taken about three times as long on my own.

Pitfalls of Partnerships

Partnerships can easily go wrong too, even when partnered with a trustworthy person. Some of the ways they can go wrong are divorce, disability, disinterest, and death. Dave Ramsey talks about these on his podcast. For example, if you and your brother partner up, and he gets a divorce, there is a possibility that his spouse is entitled to half of your brother's share of the business. If your brother doesn't have a lot of extra cash to pay off his ex-wife, then you'll likely need to sell the property in order to pay off the spouse. If you're not finished with the renovation, then you'll likely have to sell at a loss, and your whole business could be at risk.

Disinterest is where one party decides he no longer wants to be involved in the business. Assuming you have a good relationship with your partner, hopefully he would wait until the project was complete before backing out of the flip project. But, if he decides halfway through that this isn't the business for him, you are going to have to either sell the property to liquidate the funds to pay him or you'll need to come up with the funds out of your own pocket.

Another risk is that you or your partner becomes disabled. Let's say you and your partner agreed to each put in 50% of the cash and each do 50% of the labor. What happens if you become disabled and aren't able to do any additional labor? Does your partner get a bigger share of the profit because of his additional time in the project? Do you both have enough money to finish the renovation now that you are only getting disability pay instead of your whole paycheck?

Another risk when doing a partnership is death. What happens if your partner dies half way through the project? Again, no one expects this to happen, but it can happen. In this event your partner's heirs will be entitled to his share of the business. If they do not want to participate in the flip, then you will need to compensate them for your partner's share of the business equity. You will either need to sell the project partially completed, most likely for a loss in order to pay the estate or you'll need to come up with the funds to settle your partner's estate. In both cases, you may lose your flipping business. You may have the partner you trust 100%, but if divorce, disability, or death happens, it may not be controllable by your partner. Remember these risks when entering a partnership and try to insure yourself in case any of these situations arise.

To Become a Real Estate Agent or Not

I got very lucky when I found my real estate agent. To be honest I didn't do a lot of research. She happened to be the listing agent (the agent representing the seller) for my first flip property, the short sale that I purchased to live in. I found the property by visiting realtor.com, watching the price as it was reduced over and over again. I reached out to her since she was the agent already dealing with this property. Generally, you don't want your agent representing you, the buyer, and the seller at the same time. But, since this property had reduced its price so much over the previous year on the market, I thought the negotiating would be limited. I was right. I went ahead and offered the forty-nine thousand dollars that it was listed at, and after she negotiated with the bank, we were set to move forward with the sale at that price.

I was happy with the way that purchase went and ended up using her as my listing agent when I sold this property, the Elm property. She was also our buyers' agent for the Ditmore property as well as our sellers' agent when we sold it. We ended up with five offers during the sale of this property. She did a great job coordinating the multiple offer situation, and we ended up selling for a higher price than expected. Through the buying and selling of properties with her, I was able to learn a little more on each transaction. After going through the process a few times, you will start to see the patterns, understanding the steps necessary to get the deal done. Deb and I went ahead and ran some calculations, and for us, it seemed like a good option for me to become an agent and represent us. The downside to me becoming our agent is that we no longer talk to our previous agent as often as we did. We really enjoyed learning from her.

Depending on the volume of flips you do each year, it may be beneficial to get your real estate license and represent your flips when buying and selling. If you are new to real estate or have less experience, you should find a good agent and start learning as much as you can. If you have more experience and knowledge in real estate, it may be worth it to get your real estate license. Once you begin buying and selling, you will see the hefty commissions come out of your bottom line, especially when selling your properties. Sellers bear the brunt of the closing fees, usually paying out 6% to the agents (3% for the buyer's agent and 3% for the listing agent). This adds up quickly.

On the flip side, it is not cheap to become an agent. Depending on the broker, you will likely pay monthly agent fees, annual membership fees for your local and national Realtor associations, which give you access to the MLS, as well as the agent-broker commission split. In addition to the money, there is a significant time commitment required to be an agent. There are continuing education requirements and post-licensing education requirements that all take time.

In order to determine if it's a good option for you, create a budget for the number of flip properties you believe you can purchase and sell in a given year. Then, figure out how much commission you would make on each transaction. Next, talk to some real estate brokers in your area. Ask them to give you an estimate of the fees you would need to pay as an agent for their brokerage as well as the commission split percentage. Some brokers allow agents to do personal deals where they take a lower percentage and some do not.

Then, do the math. What option is better financially? Here is an example where the monthly fees are $85 per month, and the agent has an 80/20 split with the broker. This represents one flip per year. In the end this does seem logical to become an agent. However, this is not accounting for the time and the original licensing classwork or the license exam costs.

Real Estate Agent	Income (+) / Expense (-)
Realtor Association / MLS Annual Fees	$ (1,100)
Annual Broker Fees	$ (1,020)
Signs/Marketing/etc	$ (600)
Continuing Education	$ (200)
Transaction 1 - Purchase Flip for $60K @ 3%	$ 1,800
Broker %	$ (360)
Transaction 2 - Sell Flip for $130K @ 3%	$ 3,900
Broker %	$ (780)
Total*	**$ 1,640**

*Costs do not include cost of classes and exam to attain License

I personally got my real estate license because it is something I've always wanted to do, and the numbers seemed to make sense. I've always had an interest in real estate and had to give this a try. I thought we would do a bit higher volume than one per year, however, but even at one per year this is still a favorable outcome for us. Flipping property takes time. There is no value in rushing through it and doing unsatisfactory work. Working full-time and flipping on the side doesn't allow for us to do much more than one flip per year. We do most of the work ourselves and hire out only the very technical aspects, or areas where permitting requirements necessitate hiring a licensed contractor. This is our strategy, and it works for us. You may have more time to dedicate to flipping and you may hire out more projects, which could expedite your renovation time.

If you prefer to concentrate on only the renovation aspect of the flip, then don't worry about becoming an agent. There are many great agents available that can find you deals and keep you busy without you needing to worry about all of the aspects of getting the deals closed or finding the next great deal. They can focus on that and you can focus on your piece thereby allowing you to do a few flips per year.

For example, the agent we used to have is awesome. She is patient, is customer service oriented, and knows her market well. Interview multiple agents and let them know your plan upfront. Not every agent wants to participate with people flipping properties, because they know there is a lot of work ahead of them. There will be more offers written with less winning offers. Make sure the agent you choose knows your market and your price range well. If your agent does well, then they can also represent you when selling the property. Once you get the first flipped property purchased and sold, your agent will see your skills and will go the extra mile to find you excellent flipping potentials.

Figure Out Your Flipping Strategy

There are many people out there who consider themselves 'flippers', and there is a wide range of flipping strategies. Figuring out what works best for you is critical. For example, instead of a complete renovation, maybe you only do cosmetic changes to your flippers. Painting and changing out flooring should be a relatively quick flip. Finding houses that only need this cosmetic update might be your sweet spot. There are many properties that need a good clean-up, a fresh coat of paint, and carpets removed. Your profit margins may not be as big, but you'll likely get through these renovations quickly and have a higher volume of properties each year.

Scope of Work

We have tried different angles, but have a few things in common on each of the flips. We gutted the kitchens in all three properties, and actually moved the entire kitchen of the Ditmore property. We added bathrooms to two of the three flips. Adding a bathroom and replacing all of the plumbing in a property are time-consuming projects. We find that we are able to make a bit more profit by offering buyers a completely new kitchen and bathroom. Buyers want to see updated fixtures, cabinets, and counter tops. In many cases, they will pay a premium for these items. But again, the downside is it takes longer to complete bigger projects like these. It takes a bit of financial analysis and understanding of the real estate market in your area to assess whether the longer renovation is worth your time.

So far, we have stayed in the same price range when purchasing and selling the homes. The three purchase prices were between fifty and sixty thousand, and the three sales prices were between one-hundred and five and one-hundred and thirty thousand. We also spent a similar amount on all three, ranging from thirty to forty-five thousand including the closing costs. All three properties were near schools. Two were a block away from each other where the county has no permit requirements, and one was in a completely different city, which has plumbing and electrical permit requirements. Two were built in the 1950's and one was from 1906. The 1906 property had the most surprises and unexpected hits to the budget, which one would expect given the age. We are definitely learning as we go and are currently looking at higher priced properties to see if the price premium will increase.

If you've seen "Good Bones" on HGTV, you know their strategy. They buy up a block of properties in an up-and-coming area and then literally gut the entire house and create and an almost brand-new house. They generally seem to pay between four to fifty thousand for their properties and put another one to two-hundred thousand into them. They tend to make a little less profit on the first couple of properties they sell on the block, but then they seem to make a significant profit by the last few houses on the block.

You may come up with your own strategy. Instead of replacing cabinets, maybe your method is to repaint them and update the hardware only. Maybe you replace the counters, but you don't upgrade the materials. Or, maybe you are the extreme opposite and you decide you want to buy the worst houses and take them down to the studs in order to offer buyers an almost brand-new house like Mina and Karen on the Good Bones show.

Maybe you are the person who loves the older homes from 1900, and you specifically restore the older features while modernizing other features. Whichever strategy you decide is best for you, have an understanding of the scope of work you want to undertake before purchasing the property.

There are buyers in every price range. Understanding what your desired scope of work in each property is allows you to create a renovation budget as well as a forecasted sales price and profit margin for that property. By deciding ahead of time which projects should be carried out, you will be in a position to find the right properties for you. There is no right or wrong when it comes down to which projects you decide need to be done. However, there are different returns based on the projects you decide to do. For example, kitchens and bathrooms sell homes. If you end up spending all of your money on a furnace and a water heater, buyers will not give you the return you're looking for. Buyers assume the furnace and water heater works. Those should be a given. Buyers are more interested in how the property looks, how many bathrooms there are, and if the kitchen is functional and updated.

Geography

Another consideration is the area you want to flip in. So far, ours have been in smaller cities in Ohio. If we decided to go into a bigger area like Columbus, there may be more profit potential, but our commute would be a lot longer. Understanding the area or market you want to flip in is a big consideration. If you decide you want to flip in a rural area, you should plan for extra time on the market as there are likely fewer buyers. With smaller demand in a more rural area, it's important to understand a reasonable price range for these buyers. They likely won't pay two-hundred thousand dollars for a property. Don't over-improve a property. If you do, you may be keeping that property a lot longer than you anticipated. You also may not be able to sell it at the premium you expected. This same logic applies in a metro area. If you're in a neighborhood of houses selling around one-hundred and fifty thousand, then don't purchase a property for one-hundred and twenty-five thousand and put seventy-five thousand into it. To break even you would need to sell at two-hundred and ten thousand at the least to cover the real estate commissions. To make a decent profit, you would need to sell at two-hundred and fifty thousand, one-hundred thousand dollars over any other property in the neighborhood. That is a hard sale, if not an impossible sale. Be aware of the market whenever choosing a property.

Exit Plan

Most people assume that flippers buy, renovate, and sell their properties immediately after the completion of the renovation. This is true of many flippers. These flippers are trying to liquidate their flip properties at a profit in order to buy more flip properties. The benefit of this strategy is evidently the ability to get your cash out of the property. The downside is that all of this profit is taxable in the year the flip property is sold. This strategy works for many flippers. They enjoy the renovation of the projects and like finding deals. They use the profits to continue to find more deals. They have the option to put their profits back into the business, or they can transfer those profits into their personal bank accounts and use it however they feel, while still having enough funds in the business account to find another flip property.

There are other strategies for exiting flip properties though. For example, some flippers fix up their properties in order to rent them out. The flippers do not get their entire investment back immediately, but they are giving themselves future monthly cash inflows from the rent payments. The benefit of this strategy is that your taxes on the improvement of the property are generally deferred and you only pay tax on the income that the rent generates. This is generally a lower tax bill for all of the years the property is rented and not sold. If you enjoy working with tenants, don't need the initial investment back immediately, and prefer a steady stream of income versus one large profit on the sale, then renting your flip properties might be the strategy for you. If you can continue saving up the money to purchase more properties and rent them out, you may generate a stream of income big enough to quit your full-time job.

Another strategy is a hybrid of the two above. Some flippers will renovate the property, rent it out for a year, and then sell it. Reasons for this might be the real estate market, the time of year, or tax reasons. If the market is leaning towards a buyers' market, you may want to wait until the market turns towards a sellers' market where you can generally get a price premium in the sale. If you finish the renovation in the winter, you may want to rent it for six months and put it on the market during the summer for more demand. If you follow this approach, be ready to make additional repairs after your tenant leaves.

Another strategy might be you moving into the flip property when the renovation is complete. If you live in the property for at least two years, then when you sell it, you will not pay any taxes on the gain of the property, up to two-hundred and fifty thousand dollars. You can continue this pattern, renovate a property, move into it for two years, and then sell it at a non-taxable profit. There are specific rules on this. Check with your tax professional or read IRS publication 523 for more detailed information. If you decide to go with this strategy, do not put the property in an LLC name, keep it in your personal name.

Tax Implications of Your Strategy

Flipping

Another consideration when determining your flipping strategy is the tax impact it has. If you decide to purely flip properties – buy them, renovate them, and sell them – you'll simply pay taxes on the profit you make each year. We've followed this strategy on the Ditmore and Meadow properties. We formed an LLC where we each own 50% of the business. When doing an LLC, the profit of the LLC simply passes onto your personal taxes. The actual LLC does not pay any taxes. For example, if we made twenty thousand dollars in one year, Deb and I would need to show on our personal taxes that we each had an additional ten thousand dollars in income. This profit of ten thousand dollars is shown as ordinary income and is taxed at the same rate in which our full-time jobs are taxed.

You may want to get an accountant to make sure you are accounting for all of the expenses accurately and reporting everything correctly on your tax return. We use Excel to track our revenue and expenses as well as to reconcile our bank account. There are a few tax documents that need to be completed for the LLC, which we have completed by hand the last two years. And, then I use TurboTax to do my personal taxes. It's not overly complicated at our current pace. We are literally doing one flip per year, which makes it easy. If you start to do multiple flips in one year and have some partially completed flips on December 31, taxes do increase in difficulty due to having inventory at the cut-off date. If you're concerned about how to report anything, consult your tax professional.

Renting

Like I mentioned earlier, many people flip property, but instead of selling it, they rent it out after the renovation is completed. There are different strategies even within renting. For example, some individuals hold onto and accumulate many rentals for long-term renting. They are therefore deferring most of the taxable gain in the value of the property to a much later date when they will eventually sell the property. In other words, they are deferring the profit by renting. Instead of cashing in the twenty thousand dollars in profit that year, they are renting it for ten thousand dollars a year and making a smaller taxable profit in the first year, reducing their overall tax liability in that year.

Another rental strategy is to flip the property and then rent it out for one year. This means that you've owned the property for more than one year, putting it in the long-term capital gains category similar to the above paragraph. After that year of renting, let's say you sell it for the same twenty thousand dollars in profit. Instead of my share, the 50%, being taxed at my ordinary income rates which are closer to 25%-30%, this ten-thousand-dollar gain is taxed at the long-term capital gains rate of 15%, which is much lower than my ordinary income tax rate. In addition to the lower tax bill, we were also able to collect ten thousand dollars in rent in that year, but had to pay two thousand dollars for additional repairs after the tenant left. This is a smart strategy from a tax perspective. But, if you don't want the hassle of dealing with a tenant or don't want the tenant to destroy all of the work you've put into the flip property, then you may want to sell the property immediately.

Occupying

The last strategy we will discuss is making the flip property your primary residence. This is more difficult or may even be impossible if you're in a partnership with someone other than your spouse. Let's say you are doing a flip on your own. You start to fall in love with the property. You're spending many hours there and investing a lot of labor, and you decide you want to make it your primary residence. This is possible, assuming the property is in your personal name and not an LLC's name. There are tax advantages to moving into a flip property. If you live in a property for at least two years and then sell the property, you are not liable for taxes on the gain of the property. Let's say you purchased the property for fifty thousand dollars and sold it for one-hundred and ten thousand dollars. That sixty thousand difference would not be taxable. Yes, you likely spent thirty thousand dollars in renovations, but in this scenario, those would not be deductible as this is your personal residence. There aren't many loopholes like this in the tax law where you can profit up to two-hundred and fifty thousand dollars on your primary residence and not pay taxes on that profit.

This is the best strategy if you do not want to flip properties every single year and you also don't want to be a landlord. How bothered would you be to move every three-to-seven years? This is an easy way to make money in real estate and also avoid income taxes. If you want to learn more about this loophole, go to the IRS website (irs.gov), and you will find a very interesting document, Publication 523. As of tax year 2018, you can sell your home for a profit of up to $250,000 and not pay a penny in taxes on that gain. There aren't too many ways you can make a profit and keep 100% of it for yourself.

I was able to take advantage of this tax break when I sold the Elm property back in 2016. In 2012 I was hesitant to put an offer in on this property, which was a short sale property. A few years earlier, I had put an offer in on a short sale in Los Angeles, and it was painful. After months of waiting, my real estate agent communicated that they were accepting my offer. I paid for an appraisal and an inspection, and then found out that the bank foreclosed on the property, and they were putting it back on the market. After all of that waiting and paying for the appraisal and inspection, I didn't think I would ever put an offer in on a short sale property again. However, here I was, getting ready to put in another short sale offer. I had followed this property for months, watching its price go from eighty thousand to sixty thousand to forty-nine thousand dollars, where it was when I finally put the offer in. It needed a lot of TLC (tender, love, and care). I put in the offer at the end of December 2011 and closed in February 2012.

There was a lot of work that needed to be done, but I knew this was going to be a good investment. From my experience as a mortgage lender, I knew there was a tax advantage to living in a property for two years. The work seemed overwhelming at the time. However, the neighbors ended up being very nice, and the area ended up being a great location. It was near a school and baseball fields that hosted baseball games and practices almost every evening in the spring and summers.

The American Dream has primarily been to own your own home. Many people want to own their own little piece of the United

States. Real estate over the long run has almost always appreciated in value, with the exception of the 2008 recession. It's a great feeling to know that you own your own property. Many people need to work very hard to be able to afford and get approved for a mortgage, including me. It took me a lot of years in the workforce to be able to have the good credit score and enough cash for a down payment to get approved for the loan. Home ownership brings a feeling of satisfaction even if it is a lot of work in some cases, especially when buying a fixer upper. Home ownership encourages commitment to your community, as well as continual improvements to the property, and has been linked to lower crime rates. Home ownership comes with many benefits, and the US government knows this. They, therefore, offer incentives for being a home owner. Home owners can deduct their mortgage interest if they itemize their deductions. And, most importantly, home owners don't pay tax on the profit they make from selling their property at a higher price than they originally paid for it, assuming they follow the few simple conditions outlined in Publication 523.

Just a side note, generally we define profit as sales less all expenses. Because of the way the tax law considers real estate transactions in this specific publication, only the purchase price and the final sales price are the variables that the government allows you to use in this calculation. It does not include all of the expenses you incurred to update and remodel the property. Minimizing your renovation costs becomes more important in this regard. For example, if you purchased your primary residence for fifty thousand dollars and put thirty thousand into its remodel, and you sold this property for eighty thousand, you really didn't make a profit, but the IRS would see it as a gain of thirty thousand because they do not consider the extra expense you put into it. As long as it was your primary residence for at least two years, however, you would not have any tax liability on this gain. Make sure you check out IRS Publication 523 and talk to you tax professional to ensure you have a proper understanding if you want to go this route. I highly recommend taking advantage of this.

5: Find the Flip

How to Find a Good Flip Property

Finding the right property for your flip is crucial. If you aren't able to find any properties at a discount, your flipping career will never get started. In Chapter 1, I mentioned a handful of free resources to use when starting to research flipping real estate. You will see some of these free resources below. I want you to get a sense of how important some of these tools are, which is why I'm going into a bit more detail about how to use these tools and approaches when looking for deals.

Realtor & Zillow Apps

The way I start almost every flip search is to use apps like Realtor and Zillow. I don't necessarily trust the valuation on these apps, but I do trust the relative values between neighboring properties. For example, if I see a property I like on the app, I can make a very quick decision on whether or not the property has profit potential by looking at the neighboring properties. If my potential flip is for sale for one-hundred thousand dollars and all of the surrounding properties are worth one-hundred thousand dollars, there is likely no room for profit. Even if all of the properties are valued at one-hundred and ten thousand dollars, with realtor fees, there will be no profit. These don't even make my initial cut. But, if I see a property for sale at ninety-five thousand dollars and the neighbors are valued around one-hundred and fifty thousand dollars, then that may have some flip potential. When you find one of these gems, look at how long the property has been listed. If this is a high number, anything over six months, this may be a sign that the seller is more apt to negotiate the price. Also, review the Property History section. This tells you if the property has sold recently and what value it sold at. This will give you an indicator, based on the prior year and value of the last sale, how much the property has appreciated or how far off the seller is in the listing price.

I do this with as many properties as I can find, which have this difference in value compared to their neighbors. Once I have this list, the second thing I do is narrow it down by doing some more detailed analysis about the neighborhood, age of the property versus its neighbors, and size of property. I also drill down into the neighboring properties to see if there have been any recent sales. Actual selling prices are the benchmark to go by. I generally use the Realtor and Zillow apps for this step, but the MLS database makes this step easier. I'll get into that later.

County Auditor Website

The third step I do when I'm starting to get interested in a property is to visit the county auditor website. There is so much public information on this site. You can usually find the historical sale prices of this property as well as property tax information, and whether or not the owner is current on their property tax payments. You can also generally determine whether this property is being used as a rental by the owner's address. If the owner is having mail sent to a different address, they are most likely renting out the property. You can also confirm the age of the home, the size of the home, how many buildings are on the property, and if there have been any additions to the home.

Real Estate Agents & Property Managers

Another successful way to find good deals is to know agents and make sure those agents know you are looking for potential flip properties. A few months ago, an agent I know very well gave us a heads-up on a property she was getting ready to put on the market. This property was a gem. It would have been a perfect flip property and I know we could have made money on it. The problem was that a lot of people wanted this property. In the end there were five offers, many of which were all cash and no contingencies, and we landed in second place. The seller chose the person who bid the highest. I wouldn't have even known about this property if I didn't have that relationship with the real estate agent. Property managers are also in a position to know about good deals. They have relationships with current investors who might be buying or selling. Go and meet your local property managers. They are in constant communication with their investors. Once one of these contacts tells me about a potential flip, I then go and start to analyze based on the Zillow and Realtor apps as well as the county auditor website.

County Sheriff Sales (Foreclosure Auctions)

We've been to quite a few sheriff sales and I've bid many times, but have yet to win a bid at a foreclosure sale. At any auction, it's very important to set your ceiling before you get to the sale. Foreclosures at an auction come with higher risk, because you, as the buyer, may likely be responsible for some of the liens on the property. In a regular purchase, the seller is required to clear all liens before the property is transferred to the buyer, but a foreclosure auction is different. There are liens that stay with the property. This means if you purchase a property for fifty thousand dollars but there are ten thousand worth of liens which you are responsible for, in essence, you just paid sixty thousand for the property. We always set our ceiling prior to these auctions and add a higher contingency within our budget for these possible liens. This may be why we haven't won any auctions yet. All of these potential liens are public information though. Take a visit to your county's recorder office and they can usually send you in the right direction to do the necessary research on the properties. We were really interested in one property at the auction, and I took time the day before to go and do this research on the property. State rules do vary when it comes to foreclosures. Before you start bidding on properties, make sure you do some research on your state's rules.

MLS (Multiple Listing Service)

If you are a real estate agent use the MLS, and if not, have your agent do your searches for you. There are many filters in the MLS to narrow the search for properties. Our last flip was an estate sale. After someone passes, their heirs, in many cases, don't want to deal with the property. In most cases, they need the property to be sold in order to settle the estate and to receive their inheritance. The MLS allows you to filter for estate sales for example. You can also filter on REO, which is Real Estate Owned by banks. These are properties which went to a foreclosure auction, and no one bid high enough to cover the bank's costs, therefore the bank purchased the property back. In other words, you can filter for foreclosures that have already been through the auction and can now be purchased with no risk of any additional liens.

Another good filter is the number of days on market. When a property has been on the market for over six months, the owners may be more open to price negotiation. All three of the flips I've done had been on the market for more than four months.

The MLS is an excellent source of information. I mentioned previously that the MLS can quickly show recent sales in your potential area. It allows the user to search for specific properties that have been sold recently. For example, properties with two bedrooms, or properties that are less than 40 years old. There are many filters and search criteria that can quickly narrow down your analysis and give you a good perspective on what you should pay for the property based on its current condition and what you can expect to sell the property for in excellent condition. In order to have access to the MLS, you would either need to get your real estate license or request this information from your real estate agent, who can produce a report.

Local Banks

Another way to find properties for a good deal is to visit your local bank. Banks have a relatively constant flow of properties being foreclosed upon and purchased back by the bank. At the foreclosure auction you can almost always pick out the lenders. They have their lowest bid values in hand. When the borrower/owner of the property stops paying the mortgage payment, banks foreclose, which means the house goes up for sell at auction. Depending on how much equity the borrower/owner had in the property, the bank could lose a lot of money if they let the property sell for too low of a value. Therefore, they will bid up the price if no one else bids up far enough. This means they buy and own many properties. Banks aren't in the business of buying back properties. They almost always want to sell these as quickly as they can. If you get to know the lenders in your area, you might be able to pick up a property this way.

When I was a mortgage lender in my early twenties, the bank I worked at almost convinced me to purchase property from them. There was one in a decent neighborhood that most likely would have worked out, but there was a second property that I am happy I stayed away from. It was in a more questionable area, and the previous owners basically stripped everything they could out of this house. Banks are in the business of lending money; they're not property managers.

FSBO (For Sale By Owner)

Another interesting angle you may want to try is considering the properties where the owners decide to sell without a real estate agent. In the real estate world, we call these FSBO's (pronounced FIZBO's). These owners typically see the cost of commission too high and think they can end up with more money in their pockets by not using an agent. In some cases, these sellers have a bias because this is their home. They see it as much more valuable than the market regards it. In many cases it may not be worth your time to talk to these sellers, but there are always the few exceptions where the sellers just want out of the property. They might be facing foreclosure in the coming months. They might even be valuing their property lower than what the market would value it at.

While taking my real estate classes, the appraisal instructor told us this story of a man whose father had passed away. He inherited his father's property, which was located in a different city. He didn't want to pay the commissions to an agent and put the property up for sale himself. He put an ad in the local newspaper. Immediately, he received a call and sold the property to a woman who had seen the advertisement. She agreed to pay his asking price of thirty thousand dollars. This appraisal instructor was the appraiser hired to value the property. The property was appraised around one-hundred thousand dollars. The appraiser asked the seller how he came up with the price to sell the property at. He said he looked at the county auditor website and saw the tax value of the property. What he didn't realize was that this value was at 35% of the total tax value of the property. Because he didn't want to pay roughly 6% of the total sales price, he ended up losing almost seventy thousand dollars! This is an extreme example. I wouldn't expect to find this deal when reaching out to these individuals. They are likely to either have a bias of higher-than-market-value or lower-than-market-value. Without any experience in real estate, owners of FSBO's are pricing their property based on their own intuition. It may be worth having a conversation to see if there is a potentially good deal for you.

Homeowners Facing Foreclosure or Wholesalers

Another way to find a good flip property opportunity is through homeowners who are getting ready to face a foreclosure on their home. Generally, you'll hear the term 'wholesaler' when trying to purchase a property this way. A wholesaler is someone who scouts through the local newspapers and on the local county sheriff sale website to see which homes are going to the foreclosure auctions in the coming months. Once this wholesaler finds a potential home to buy, he must convince the homeowners to sell it to him before the foreclosure auction. This can be harder than it sounds. Many people are unwilling to accept that their home is about to be foreclosed upon. This is definitely an emotional event as their homes are about to be taken from them. They may not have a place to go or an apartment lined up. Some homeowners may have a plan to make catch-up payments to the bank before the actual auction happens. Wholesalers have a talent in teaching the homeowner their options. No one ever wants to experience a foreclosure. If the homeowners really can't afford the payments, selling their house to a wholesaler might be a win-win situation for both the homeowner and the wholesaler. This allows them to avoid having to go through a foreclosure, and if they had any equity in their property, they might end up with some cash at the closing.

Once a wholesaler has convinced a homeowner to sell his property, the next job of the wholesaler is to find a buyer for the property. Many wholesalers never actually purchase the property and put it in their names. Instead, they line up the seller and the buyer, being the middleman in the transaction. They generally make around five thousand per property, if they can convince the owner to sell and also find a buyer in the short time frame before the foreclosure auction. Good wholesalers have a network of real estate investors they can reach out to when they do reach a deal with the homeowner. You can either get to know a few wholesalers in your area, or you can play the role of a wholesaler by looking up properties that are about to be foreclosed upon and convince the homeowners that it's better for them to sell to you versus going through the struggles of a foreclosure. There are many books available on this topic if you want to learn more about wholesaling.

Advertisements

The final method I've become familiar with are advertisements that say you buy houses. You've seen those signs along the road or may have even received a flyer stating, "I buy houses" or "I buy houses in any condition" or "all cash, quick closing". There is generally a short phrase eluding to someone wanting to buy your house and his phone number. This is a cheap way to collect leads for potential flip properties. I've not tried this method myself, but it does appear to work.

All of the above methods of finding your next flip property need to be continually worked, figuring out which methods work best for you. If you want to transition flipping into a full-time career, you'll need properties in the pipeline at all times. You remember the cash flow phasing of a flip project, right? There is a significant delay between the time you purchase the property and the time you sell the property, which needs to be filled with cash inflows from somewhere. By consistently working these channels of finding flip properties, you will continue to have a pipeline of work and cash flow.

Location, Location, Location

When considering all of the information from above, remember that location is the factor that matters most when finding potential flip properties. You may find the best deal in the rough end of the city, but if there is no other flipping activity or potential gentrification planned, then you will likely have a difficult time selling the property. Don't get so caught up in the deal that you forget about selling the property. Always remember that selling the property at the end of your project is your number one goal. This is your exit strategy and gives you liquidity in order to purchase another one. If you can't sell your renovated property at the end of the project, you're likely stuck waiting before you can flip another one. The longer it's on the market, the more likely you'll need to decrease the price, netting a lower profit. In addition to the impact on the sales price, you'll also continue paying all of those overhead costs, including mortgage interest, property taxes, insurance, and utilities.

We didn't know the area of the Meadow property as well as we knew the area of the first two. We made a gut decision based on the proximity to a school and the curb appeal of the neighbors. After a month of demo, we had a visit from a co-worker who informed us that we purchased on the wrong side of the street. Properties on the other side of the street were in the 'nice' area, but we were literally on the other side of the street that started the less attractive area. Once she gave us this information, we thought we might have made a mistake. After she pointed this out, we could see what she had described. All properties on the other side were nice and sold for premium prices. The neighbors on the other side of our property did maintain their home, but looking further down the street, they started to progressively get in worse in condition. We were still able to sell the property within twenty-four hours of putting it on the market, but it definitely concerned us that we were on the 'wrong' side of the street. Knowing these invisible lines in neighborhoods is information you need to know when purchasing a property.

Don't do what we did in this new market. We got lucky, but I don't think we would get lucky every time. Know your area and find out where these invisible borders are by the locals in the area. Location is everything when buying and selling a property.

Learn the Permit Requirements of the Area

Permit requirements change from county to county. We've had properties in two neighboring counties in Ohio. In the first two properties there were no requirements for permits. In the next county over, where the Meadow flip was, there were requirements for electric and plumbing. In the Ditmore flip we added a bathroom and moved a kitchen. With these two projects we ended up replacing almost 100% of the original plumbing in the house. My dad did most of this plumbing work for us. He's not a licensed contractor, but is an experienced handyman. On the other hand, in the Meadow flip, we added a bathroom and moved all of the fixtures in the existing bathroom. This county required us to hire a, not only licensed plumber, but also an approved plumber by the county. We found a good company and were able to make these changes. The difference was that hiring this plumbing company was around three thousand dollars more than having my dad do the work. By understanding the permit requirements of your county, you'll get a better feel for the cost of making certain improvements.

Many of these permit requirements can be found online. Deb made a lot of calls into these permit offices to confirm we were getting the right permits in place for the work we planned to do. Many of these county offices are decent to work with and will explain the requirements pretty well to newbies in the area.

6: Purchase the Property

Don't over-pay

Make Your Money at the Buy

When it comes to real estate, I've heard so many people say, "the profit is made at the buy, not at the sell." This is the truth! I've experienced this quite a few times. When I purchased my first property back in 2009, the duplex, I didn't know this rule and had no experience buying property. I was so excited to have my first rental that I didn't think about looking up the historical sales prices of this property or look at comparable sales in the neighborhood. I negotiated with the seller a little bit, but ended up paying too much for the property. What I should have done is paid more attention to the comparable properties in the area. Today, you can also use the auditor website or you can use the Realtor and Zillow apps to find this information. Had I taken some more time to research this duplex, I may have been able to either bring the seller down further on price or I may have chosen to find another property.

I can't stress enough how important it is to not overpay for your flip property. If you overpay, it's going to be very difficult to make any money whatsoever on the property. What do I mean by overpay? If you consider the ARV of the property or your future estimated sales price of the property and your estimated costs of renovation, you'll want to add in the purchase price and ensure that this expected profit is a healthy return on investment, or at least 20%. I know I illustrated this formula earlier, but it is so important in flipping that you do not overpay that I'm showing it again.

(ARV − ARV*6% Real Estate Commissions − $4,000 − Purchase Price Ceiling − Renovation Cost) / ARV = > 20%

Be Able to Walk Away from a Deal & Have Patience

It is exciting to want to jump into a property and get started immediately. This is normal, but rushing into a property won't help you in the long run. Patience in finding your first flip is critical. If you rush into a property without considering all of the tips in this book and your additional research, you will not make as much profit, and there is a very good possibility that you will lose money. You will likely look at a minimum of ten to twenty houses before the right flip potential comes your way. Not every seller is willing to accept a lower price for his property, and not every property is in the right condition to be a good flip candidate. You must be prepared to walk away from every deal. Even if you have invested time visiting the property, writing offers, and preparing a budget for this property, you have to walk away if the seller won't budge on price. It's much better to lose some of your time than to spend months and months working on a property you paid too much for which has no chance of making a profit.

Don't Get Emotionally Attached

As you're looking at these properties, don't get emotionally attached to any of them. If you get attached, your emotions will take over and you'll make offers with your heart instead of your head. Flipping is a business. There are many properties out there available. Don't let one throw your entire plan down the drain. Once you find a couple potential flip properties, determine how much it will cost to improve the property and how much the property will sell for after the repairs are completed. Like we went through before, you will be able to come up with your targeted profit margin and your purchase price ceiling, how much you are willing to pay for this property. Once you have that number, stick to that number. Don't let the excitement of a bidding war or a negotiation game allow you to increase that value. When you came up with this budget and ceiling price, you weren't in an emotional, competitive state. When you're bidding against others or even just going back and forth with the seller, things can heat up quickly. Your competitive juices might start flowing. But, if you have your numbers set ahead of time, you'll know where your ceiling is. Don't pass it.

Deb and I are very conservative. This means we do not win a lot of offers, but we also don't over-pay. We are okay losing offers. We've been to the sheriff sales many times, and I generally participate in the bidding, but we have an ugly winning record at these sales as we have never been able to purchase a foreclosure. Before I became a real estate agent, we worked with an agent who we got along with very well. She knows her market and always had insight on the properties with the most flipping potential. We were probably difficult clients for her as we always bid low. There were multiple times where there were multiple offers on a property. She always had patience with us and knew there was a risk of losing a lot of deals. We stuck to our determined purchase price ceilings and did finally win a couple.

Another way we try to purchase the property at a discount is by enticing the seller to sell us the property by having a solid offer with no chance of the deal falling through. We almost always bid all cash with no contingencies, meaning we aren't going to cancel the deal if the inspection comes up negative. We never require an appraisal, and because we are paying with all cash, there is no risk of the financing getting disrupted. The problem is that a lot of flippers are paying all cash these days, which doesn't make our offer stand out. In some cases, the seller is willing to go through the risk of inspection and financing in order to get a higher price. We've lost at least two deals where there were multiple bids, and the seller ended up going with the higher price, which was above our purchase price ceiling.

Budget Conservatively

As I've mentioned a few times previously, be conservative when you budget. It's almost impossible to know every issue that will come up during the renovation. Even being conservative, Deb and I have spent more on all three flips than we originally expected.

Here is an example of a budget we put together for a potential flip property. You'll see there are a lot of spend categories below, but each of the lines don't go into much detail. For example, the flooring line shows a non-bathroom lump sum value of thirty-five hundred dollars. There were additional calculations that got us to this value. We took the square feet of the house less the bathroom square feet multiplied by the price per square foot to come up with this value. You'll likely do similar calculations for each of the lines.

Most of the budgets we put together look similar to this one. We start with this blank template that lists all of these spend categories to ensure we do not forget any. You will find that you will tend to spend money on the same areas house after house, assuming you are finding properties in similar condition. For us, we tend to spend more in the kitchen and bathrooms than anywhere else. All houses are slightly different in their maintenance and renovation needs, but the overall concept stays consistent for us.

You will also notice below that we have two columns: high and low. When estimating the future sales price of the property or ARV, it is very difficult to know exactly what price the property will be sold for. We determine a range in which we believe the property will be sold for. In the example below, we assumed the property would sell for between one-hundred and two thousand to one-hundred and eleven thousand dollars. We create a low scenario where we would spend less on the renovation and therefore would likely sell it for less. This gives us a lower purchase price ceiling. We also look at the high scenario to see how much we could increase our purchase price ceiling if we spent a little more on the renovation and were able to sell it for the higher value. As a side note, these numbers are all assumptions based on the information we know about this flip property and the comparable properties we have looked up using the MLS or the county auditor website.

We use a simple Microsoft Excel sheet for our flip budgeting template. There are other tools available, but Excel is free, assuming you've already got it installed on your computer, and it's easy to use. You'll notice we have shaded and unshaded values. The shaded values are formula driven, meaning these are calculated based off of the numbers that are not shaded, which are input values. By making several assumptions with the unshaded values, the shaded values will calculate, making it easy to change assumptions and get a new output. This is the best tool for us and works well for us.

Budget		Low	High
	Sales Price	$ 102,000	$ 111,000
6%	Real Estate Commission	$ (6,120)	$ (6,660)
	Buyer Closing Costs	$ (3,000)	$ (3,000)
	Other Closing Costs (title insurance, recording, etc)	$ (1,000)	$ (1,000)
	Net Price	**$ 91,880**	**$ 100,340**
	Purchase Price Ceiling	**$ (50,000)**	**$ (55,000)**
	Operating Costs		
	Exterior		
	Roof	$ -	$ -
	Garage Repair	$ (500)	$ (500)
	Outdoor paint / sandpaper / kaulk	$ (1,200)	$ (1,200)
	Power Wash / Vinyl Siding / Wood Siding repair	$ (50)	$ (50)
	Landscape	$ (200)	$ (200)
	Kitchen		
	Kitchen cabinets	$ (2,000)	$ (2,400)
	Kitchen appliances	$ (2,000)	$ (2,400)
	Kitchen counters	$ (1,800)	$ (1,800)
	Kichen other (pulls, lights, backsplash, sink, faucet)	$ (1,000)	$ (1,000)
	Bathroom		
	Shower/Shower door	$ (1,000)	$ (1,200)
	Vanity/Faucets	$ (600)	$ (800)
	Plumbing/Toilet	$ (200)	$ (200)
	Other (lighting, mirror, shelves)	$ (150)	$ (250)
	Walls		
	Indoor paint / sandpaper / kaulk / screws	$ (800)	$ (800)
	Doors (interior & exterior)	$ (400)	$ (600)
	Trim/baseboards/quarter-round	$ (1,000)	$ (1,000)
	Flooring		
	Bathroom Flooring (tile/cement board/grout)	$ (300)	$ (500)
	Non-bathroom Flooring (laminate)	$ (3,500)	$ (4,000)
	Utility		
	Furnace	$ -	$ -
	Hot Water Heater	$ -	$ -
	Electric (wire, boxes, outlets, switches)	$ (500)	$ (500)
	Permits	$ -	$ -
5%	Contingency	$ (3,360)	$ (3,720)
	Total Operating Costs	**$ (20,560)**	**$ (23,120)**
	Overhead Costs		
	Utilities (9 months)	$ (945)	$ (945)
	Trash (9 months)	$ (360)	$ (360)
	Property Taxes (9 months)	$ (975)	$ (975)
	Insurance (9 months)	$ (675)	$ (675)
	Total Overhead Costs	**$ (2,955)**	**$ (2,955)**
	Total Costs	**$ (73,515)**	**$ (81,075)**
	Potential Profit	**$ 18,365**	**$ 19,265**
	Return	**20%**	**19%**

Sales Price

The Sales Price section is related to the future sale of the property when you have finished the renovation. You'll notice the first line within this section is the sales price. This is what some call the ARV or the value after all of the repairs are completed. In order to come up with this number, you'll need to either work with a good real estate agent or do this yourself. You can use the Realtor and Zillow apps or the MLS database to see the sold prices of comparable homes. For example, if this budget was for a three-bedroom, two bath property, then look for three-bedroom, two bath homes in the area that have sold recently. This is a much easier task to do in the MLS database. You'll also want to find similarly aged and sized properties for this comparison. If you do not have access to the MLS database, request this from your real estate agent. This is important information as it will direct the other calculations in the template. In addition to looking at similarly sized and aged homes, you will want to check out the neighbors' most recent sales prices. During this phase spend most of your time looking up recent sales prices. Estimates are not what you want during this phase; you need to see actual, historical sale prices. These will be the most telling in how you determine this property's future estimated sales price.

If the neighbors all have significantly different sales prices, compare the size and age of the neighbors' properties to your potential flip property. If most of them have an additional bedroom, then you'll need to subtract some of the value from this potential flip. In order to determine how much an extra bedroom or an extra bathroom is valued at, look at more historical sales prices. These values differ greatly depending on your specific location and market.

The next line represents the real estate commissions. The seller almost always covers these for both the seller and the buyer. These are usually 3% for each agent. This cost will, therefore, depend on the sales price. If you start using the same agent multiple times a year, you may get to a point where these fees could be negotiated. However, don't expect to negotiate this on the first deal you do with an agent. 3% is standard, and most agents will stick to this percentage.

The next line represents the buyer's closing costs. These are the costs that you, as the seller, can decide how much to extend to the buyer to cover his closing costs. These are completely negotiable with the buyer. In the first two flips we did, we ended up giving up three thousand dollars to each of those buyers. In this third flip the initial offer did not include any of the buyer's closing costs, but by the final round of offers he included one thousand of his closing costs for us to cover. The reason we will agree to cover part of the buyer's closing costs is because we flip properties in a lower price range, where our buyers are usually first-time homeowners. They are already having trouble coming up with the 10% to 20% down payment. If we can help them out by covering some of the additional funds they need to come up with for the closing, then we can manage this. This is why we always assume we will cover three thousand dollars of the buyer's closing costs.

The final row in this section is other closing cost, which consists of the title insurance, the recording fee, a property tax true-up, and some other miscellaneous fees that the title company charges to close the sale. These fluctuate based on state and especially on sales price of the property. Generally, one thousand covers us for properties in Ohio in the mid-one-hundred thousand range.

Add these four lines together, and this is your net sales price or your net revenue when the sale is finalized. By having an idea of what this value will be plus the renovation costs, you'll be able to determine how much you should pay to purchase this flip property. Remember this equation? You've just determined the ARV and can now calculate the ARV*6%.

(ARV − ARV*6% Real Estate Commissions − $4,000 − Purchase Price Ceiling − Renovation Cost) / ARV => 20%

Purchase Price

The Purchase Price represents the maximum price you will pay for the flip property or your purchase price ceiling. I leave this row blank until I have filled in all of the other values. By determining the future sales price and the renovation budget (operating & overhead costs), you now have all of the right information to come up with the maximum price you are willing to pay for the property. The guideline we use is we want to at least have a 20% margin. To get the margin %, use the formula above. This Purchase Price ceiling becomes a plug number, meaning once you have all of the other values filled in, you can adjust this number up and down until you get to the 20% minimum. In the above example, we would likely not offer higher than fifty thousand dollars for this property. This is the Low column. It appears even though we may be able to sell this property for the higher future sales price, paying fifty-five thousand might cut our margin percentage too thin.

Operating Costs

The renovation budget needs to cover all of the items you plan to change, replace, and improve in the property. The above budget is a sample of one of our budgets. We put together a similar template for every property we look at as a potential flip candidate. We have put together a countless number of these budgets as we have looked at a lot of properties. Yes, that's correct, we've only completed three flips, but we have put together at least fifty of these budgets. Not every property is a good flip candidate. The more experience you have analyzing properties, the more accurate you will get. As illustrated, a lot of research goes into finding the right house. By reading this book, it's clear you're doing your research.

The above template is what we use, but it may not encompass everything that needs to be improved in your property. Be flexible in adding items or removing items depending on the property needs. As you complete more budgets and figure out your flipping strategy, you'll know exactly what line items need to be added and completed. Also, as you complete more flips, you will see the actual costs of these items. There are always items we miss. For example, sometimes one box of drywall screws isn't enough, or you need more dust masks than expected. These are small and generally don't make or break the budget. It's important to add as many items as you can though as these small items will add up if enough of them are missed. You can look up most prices online, which is a quick and easy resource. Some of the major items are described below.

1. Exterior (Roof, Paint or Siding, Driveway Concrete or Gravel, Outdoor Building Repair, Landscape)

Roof

We have been lucky in that we have never had to purchase a new roof for a flip property. Roofs are expensive. If you know a property needs a new roof, try to get estimates from multiple vendors before you put in an offer. This is a significant cost, and if you don't budget for this properly, you could be sinking all of your potential profit into a new roof.

Paint or Siding

Most properties that are potential flip properties have not had their exterior maintained throughout the years. We've had different exterior treatments for all three properties. The Elm property needed new siding. This was expensive, costing around fifteen thousand dollars. Again, similar to the roof, you'll need to make the decision on whether you purchase new siding prior to your offer as this will dictate your purchase price ceiling value significantly. The Ditmore property had cedar siding on it, which was rotting in some spots. We also removed an exterior doorway in this property and needed to replace that doorway with the same cedar siding. We were able to find a replacement cedar siding at Lowes and used this to replace the rotting spots as well. We then finished this exterior by painting it. With the exterior paint and additional siding, we had around one thousand dollars in this project. The Meadow property had vinyl siding already; it just hadn't been cleaned in years. Deb's dad power washed it for us, and it looked great.

There are many conditions and materials that can be used for exteriors, including vinyl and cedar siding, stucco, brick, and cinder block. Figure out what repairs are required and find the best-looking solution for your flip. No matter which you choose, make sure it looks clean. Having a positive first impression of a house will make your flip a more attractive purchase to potential buyers.

Driveway Concrete or Gravel

We were lucky on two of the flips that they didn't need much in the way of driveway repair, however the Ditmore driveway needed a lot of help, something we had not budgeted. The original driveway was paved, but it was only around eight feet wide. We could barely get two cars in the drive way, one behind the other, without the cars sticking out into the street. If any family with more than one car was going to buy this property, we knew the driveway needed to be at least twenty feet wide in order for two cars to fit side by side. We hired an excavation company, and they were able to dig out the twenty feet as well as remove the original pavement. We ended up using gravel in the new driveway. It looked very nice and was much more functional. Always think about the buyer when you're picking the projects to do on the flip property. If something is inconvenient for you, as the flipper, then you know the homeowner who lives here 24/7 will also be inconvenienced by it as well.

Outdoor Building Repair

The Ditmore property was the property consumed with trash when we purchased it. There was a shed in the backyard that was filled with trash and appeared that it might fall over at any moment. Again, no buyer wants a shed that might fall over at any given moment. We knew we needed to demolish and remove this shed completely. We invited a couple friends over and had a great time taking down this shed. With a flip property, you never know who in your friend-network might be helpful. Some of your friends, who you might never have expected, would actually love to help demolish an outdoor shed or kitchen cabinets. The friend who helped us demo the shed was someone who had never operated a saw before, but she got right in there and sawed away at this building. It was fun and entertaining, and she contributed a lot.

The Meadow property had a garage-like building in the backyard, which also appeared to be in bad shape. It had been damaged badly by termites and rot. We hired an exterminator and ended up keeping this building. We reinforced it by sistering all of the rotten rafters and replaced the center beam holding most of the weight. It wasn't a complete remodel, but we did enough work to ensure the building was sturdy and could be used for storage.

Everyone needs extra storage these days. If you can save an outdoor building, do it. If the existing buildings have passed the point of being saved, remove them and replace them with something functional.

Landscape

Curb appeal is likely the first thing a potential buyer will see when searching for a house to buy. By improving the roof, exterior walls, and outdoor buildings, you will significantly improve the look of the property. Don't forget about the landscaping as well. Depending on the area of the country you're in, you may need to completely replace the sod. Or, in our case, we needed to mow every week during the summers. The most significant landscaping we have done is removing untenable bushes and trees. All three flip landscapes had been ignored for a long time. In one case, medium sized trees were growing inches from the house. We decided to remove these trees and bushes ourselves. Deb would initially use her tool, a chain saw, to remove the biggest parts of the bushes. I, then, used my tools, a shovel and an ax, to dig out and cut down these trunks and stumps. There may not have been a need to dig these stumps completely out of the ground, but again, if the stump is completely dug out, then the future homeowner will not have to worry about hitting it when mowing the yard.

Landscaping, for us, wasn't a major expense, but it was a decently sized piece of the labor and time we spent at the flip properties. Make sure you add in time for this on your main timeline. And, if you're digging with a shovel, be prepared for not only a strenuous workout, but also some nasty blisters.

2. Kitchen (Counters & Backsplash, Cabinets & Pulls, Appliances, Lighting)

If you decide to gut the kitchens of the properties you flip, you'll get familiar with the options and expenses very quickly. All three of the flips we've done have had brand new kitchens. In the Ditmore flip, we actually changed the layout completely and moved the kitchen to another part of the house. Kitchens tend to be the most expensive room when improving a property. Buyers want a new, clean, and fresh kitchen, and kitchens significantly help to sell homes. Therefore, it's critical to get it right and spend a few extra dollars in this room. The main expenses for kitchen renovations are listed below.

Counters & Backsplash

There are a wide variety of options when it comes to counters that meet any budget. For example, you can pay as low as two-hundred dollars for laminate counters to as high as you want to spend. We've gone with butcher block in two of the three properties, and I used granite in the first property. The butcher blocks come in almost any type of wood and are relatively cheap compared to other solid surfaces. They look amazing and aren't difficult to maintain. Granite was a bit more expensive, but it made that Elm property kitchen stand out. There are many different solid surfaces you can go with at many different price points. Some of these include Corian, marble, granite, and quartz. Do some research on the Internet and visit some vendors to see all of your options. You can always purchase from the large retailers or you can find a discount store and save some cash this way.

When choosing the counters, you will likely want to choose a backsplash around the same time, as these two patterns or colors need to work well together. Backsplashes can be as cheap as a couple hundred dollars to as expensive as a couple thousand dollars, depending on the tile you choose. Get a rough measurement of the square footage of the area you want to cover with backsplash to understand how much each type of tile will cost in total.

Cabinets & Pulls

There are so many options when it comes to cabinets. Again, start to visit retailers to see all of the options and price levels. You'll need to have an idea of how many cabinets you want to install and what sizes you're planning to install. Because we specialize in the lower-priced homes, we generally go to Home Depot or Lowes and get the stock white shaker cabinets. They are clean, modern, and look great. They are also priced very well. When it comes to determining how many cabinets your kitchen should have, consider how much storage the buyer will need as well as not over-crowding the kitchen with cabinets. There is a balance with how the cabinets are laid out. Will you use upper cabinets or only lower? Will you have an island with storage or no? We have not installed an island yet. Islands make sense in some homes, but they can also make a small kitchen look even smaller. We have used upper cabinets in all three properties with a combination of open shelving.

The cabinet pulls really define the look you're going for. We usually purchase these from Lowes or Home Depot, but go with a higher-priced pull. We go with something modern and simple. We really like the brushed nickel look, but I know gold is starting to become a trend. Pulls are one area where we splurge a little in the budget, because they will either complement the look and improve it or they will drag it down.

Appliances

Deb and I go back and forth about providing a refrigerator to the buyers, but so far, we have always provided the refrigerator, stove, dish washer, and microwave. It makes the kitchen look finished to have all of the appliances in place and installed. And, it is a convenience we can offer to the buyer, which helps the properties sell more quickly. We have purchased these sets from Home Depot or Lowes for the past three flips. Towards the end of the flip, we start paying attention to the local sales at these stores. They tend to have appliance sales every few months. We usually get between 20% and 35% off when we purchase these. Don't go too cheap on the appliances though as you want to provide quality products to the buyers. We have purchased stainless steel sets for all three properties as these seem to be the most popular with buyers, and they match the cabinet pulls as well as the sink faucet.

Lighting

No one wants a dark kitchen. Find a way to bring in as much natural light as possible. In all three of the flips we were able to remove a wall in the kitchen to bring in more natural light. Deb feels strongly about the lighting in the kitchen, and therefore we have had a combination of recessed lights as well as hanging lights in the kitchens we've done. Again, stick with the same tones you've been using on the other hardware. For example, we stay with brush nickel for all of the lighting as well.

3. Bathrooms (Shower & Shower Doors, Vanity & Sink, Lighting, Mirror, Toilet)

Bathrooms typically are the second highest expensive rooms in flipping. This is true for us as well. In the Ditmore and Meadow flips, we actually added a new bathroom to both properties in order to give the buyers two bathrooms. In the Meadow flip we were able to reconstruct the layout to give the buyer a master suite. Bathrooms can get pricey, depending on the showers and vanities you choose.

Shower & Shower Doors

If you decide to replace the shower in your flip property, there are a couple options. You can tile the shower enclosure or you can purchase the premade walls and base. In both cases, they aren't cheap. You can easily have one thousand to three thousand dollars in a new shower, shower doors, and shower head. We have not tried to tile a shower yet, but it is on our to-do list for the next flip property we buy. The look of the tiled shower is modern and clean. We have added the premade walls and base to the showers we've installed. They are still expensive, but do give a clean look. Glass shower doors also modernize the space. A clean, new shower, no matter which materials are used is what the buyer is looking for. Make sure the showers are clean and ensure the drains are working properly. In the last two flips we've done, nearly 100% of the plumbing was completely replaced, giving the buyers peace of mind that there shouldn't be any plumbing issues in the near future.

Vanity & Sink

Vanities are expensive as well, especially if you want to add a double sink to a bathroom. You can find nice, less expensive vanities at Lowes and Home Depot, or you can check out some websites like Wayfair and Overstock to see what else is available. On our last property we were able to add a nicer vanity which was around eight hundred dollars. When choosing a vanity, make sure there is plenty of storage either in the vanity or in the bathroom itself. Also, make sure the vanity fits appropriately in the space. You don't want to create a ten-inch spot the homeowner has to squeeze through to get to the toilet. Similar to islands in a kitchen, vanities can make a bathroom feel small too. We had an oddly shaped bathroom in the Ditmore property, which required us to find a vanity with a very narrow depth. We were able to find the right size which didn't create issues when walking through the bathroom.

Also, when budgeting, remember that faucets are almost always sold separately. These are usually around one hundred dollars each, and you'll need to purchase these for the shower as well.

Lighting, Mirror, Toilet

No one wants to get ready in a dim bathroom. If you can get natural light into the bathroom, do it. We've had a couple bathrooms without natural light. In order to make up for these, we've added two lights to the bathrooms: one above the mirror and one on the ceiling. Ensure your lighting choices tie into your faucet choices.

Similarly, with your mirror, ensure it's the appropriate size for someone to get ready. Also ensure it matches the design you are going for as well as position it at the right height.

Toilets don't generally make up much of the cost in a bathroom, as you can usually get one for around two hundred dollars. But make sure you replace the toilet. An old toilet can really bring down a bathroom's appeal.

4. Walls (Drywall, Paint, Trim & Baseboards, Doors)

Depending on the condition of your flip property, the walls may need extensive work or maybe very little. Walls are generally constructed of drywall, plaster and lathe, or paneling. This is where understanding your plan is important. Your planned projects will guide you in how much money to spend on updating the walls, trim and baseboard. We've dealt with different types of walls in all three properties, and the budgets have been different in all three. Once you decide which wall or ceiling surfaces will need to be replaced, measure roughly how many pieces of drywall you expect to use and multiply this by the price per sheet. Assume you are going to use at least two buckets of mud per room and a roll of tape, both the mesh tape for flat surfaces and the solid tape for corners, if you are replacing all of the drywall. Also, don't forget to budget for trim and baseboards. These are usually sold by the foot. Get a rough estimate of how many feet you will be replacing.

The Ditmore property had drywall on the walls. There was a bit of mudding and cleaning up in all of the bedrooms as the previous owner must have had a thousand nail holes in the walls. These weren't too bad to patch, but by moving the kitchen and creating a bathroom, we had quite a bit of new drywall to install. Don't under-estimate the time and cost of new drywall, mud, tape, and sand paper. In addition, we painted the entire house, spending at least four hundred dollars on paint. This is probably surprising too, but getting decent baseboards and trim is expensive. We spent over a thousand dollars on new baseboards and quarter-round molding throughout the house.

The Meadow property was much older than the other flips, and the walls were made of plaster and lathe. We removed many of these walls, which was a very dusty mess. We also ended up replacing ceilings in three of the rooms, almost all of the trim and baseboards, and all of the interior doors. Baseboards, trim, drywall, doors, and paint amounted to more than six thousand dollars at this property. We left the original trim in two of the rooms and wanted to match that trim in the rest of the house in order to make the house consistent overall, but this meant buying very tall and expensive trim and baseboards. We wanted the old and new parts of the house to be seamless, and I think we pulled this off, but it was expensive.

5. Flooring (Tile, Laminate, Backer Board)

Floors are another significant cost. There are many types of flooring materials to choose from, making this a difficult category. In my first property, I was lucky in that most of the home already had excellent hardwood floors, just covered by carpet. The only costs for these floors were my time and labor, and the cost of renting a sander, stain, and polyurethane. In both the Ditmore and Meadow flips, we tiled all of the bathrooms with a wood-look tile. Bathrooms need to have waterproof flooring in order to avoid mold in the future. Tile is a great option as well as a luxury vinyl tile. If you decide to use tile, remember you will need to use a cement board or backer board to ensure the floors are solid and level. To budget for these items, determine the square footage of the bathrooms and decide how many pieces of backer board and how many tiles you will need to cover the area. Remember to add in the cost of a box of screws for the backer board and the cost of spacers as well as at least one bag of thin set mortar and a bag of grout.

For the remainder of both properties we used a laminate flooring which we were able to get a good deal on. We used the same laminate throughout the entire house to let the rooms flow together. This technique really does improve the overall look of the house and improves the flow through the house. Again, you'll want to get an estimate of the square footage of the home minus the square footage of the bathrooms, assuming you are using a different flooring for the bathrooms. We usually buy about 10% extra in case some of the cuts made on the tile or the laminate reduce the ability to cover the entire space. This eliminates the risk of having to stop in the middle of the project and take a trip to the store, or in a worse scenario, ordering additional flooring which would halt the entire project for some time. Take this square footage you are planning to purchase multiplied by the price per square foot to come up with your total flooring budget.

Some laminates or hardwoods require a pad between the existing flooring and the new pieces. This pad would represent additional cost that need to be considered when budgeting. Some brands come with this padding already installed on the laminate, which is what we have purchased in the past. It saves time in laying out the pad and then laying out the flooring. We can, instead, do these two steps in one.

6. Utility (Furnace, Air Conditioner, Water Heater, Electric Box & Wire, Permits)

Although these utility items don't have a tangible impact on the design of your flip property, they are important to a buyer. Buyers want to be able to depend on their furnace, air conditioner, water heater, and electric. No one wants to deal with a cold shower, breakers constantly shutting off, and no heat. Generally, replacing these items don't add as much value to your return, but if they need to be replaced, then they need to be replaced. Most of these replacements will need to be handled by a licensed contractor. If you know your potential flip property is going to need these items to be replaced, start getting quotes as soon as you can, and ensure these items are in the budget. We made the mistake of thinking that the furnace in the Meadow flip was going to work. One winter day while we were working, the furnace just shut off and never came back on. We called a company and they said we could either replace a part on this very old furnace, which meant other parts may potentially break in the future or we could replace the entire furnace. It was nine-hundred dollars to replace the part or four thousand dollars to replace the entire furnace. We went ahead and replaced the furnace. I'd rather have it fixed for good versus having a risk that the old clunker might crash right after the buyers move in. This was another budget item that we didn't expect, but it was worth fixing.

A beneficial aspect of replacing these items is that newer equipment is more efficient than the old equipment. For example, we replaced the water heater in the Ditmore property with a tankless water heater, saving electricity and space in the utility room.

Electric can add up, especially if you are rewiring most of the house. Deb is an excellent electrician and almost completely rewired the Ditmore and Meadow properties. Wire can add up quickly. It is expensive. If you're planning to update the electric or add more lights and outlets, make sure to add the wire, outlets, switches, boxes, and covers to your budget.

The final piece of the utilities are the permitting requirements of your area. Do some research prior to purchasing the property. Make sure you have a good understanding of what will need to be permitted and how much that permitting costs. Depending on the changes you are planning to make, some permits are more expensive than others. In the county we just finished the flip in, each of the permits were managed by different offices. Deb talked to a couple of those offices to ensure we were following the local requirements. You may have something similar, where you will need to call a few people to get an accurate picture of your requirements. These individuals can likely give you the cost of each permit as well. In our case, the plumbing company we hired included this permit cost in their invoice to us.

7. Contingency

You'll see there is also a row for contingency which is a formula-driven value. We usually add in a 5% contingency to our renovation budget. This is 5% of the total cost of the property, including the purchase price ceiling value plus the value of the costs above this row (exterior, kitchen, bathroom, walls, flooring, utility). 5% has worked for us so far. We have still gone over budget on spending in all three properties though. However, we have also been able to sell at a value higher than what we originally expected. If you prefer to put an absolute value in this field, for example, five thousand dollars, instead of a percentage, that is fine too. Find the value or percentage that works for you.

Overhead Costs

Don't forget about all of the costs of maintaining the property, utilities (water, electricity, gas, trash), property taxes, mortgage interest, HOA, and property insurance. Many of these items are billed monthly or quarterly. None of them improve the property but they are necessary in order to maintain the property while you are working on it. We have avoided paying for trash by using our personal trash service to take the trash. The issue with this is that we have to haul the trash to our houses as we get it. In some cases, it seems easier to rent a dumpster, but that would be an extra five-hundred dollars at least. We try to save in any way we can.

Depending on your area, you may also need the yard mowed every week. We do this ourselves with an old mower I've had for years. We leave the lawn mower in an outdoor storage area at the flip property. If it were to ever be stolen, it wouldn't be that big of a loss. If we didn't do this ourselves, this would be another overhead cost that we would need to pay. You may need to add this to your budget.

I mentioned this earlier, but the longer it takes you renovate your flip property, the more you'll pay in all of these categories. Property taxes can add up quickly and can be very expensive depending on your area. The quicker you can complete the renovation, the less you will spend on these overhead items.

Return

The final number on our budget is the return on investment percentage (or the margin percentage). We are always striving for this number to be at least 20%. If we can get to a reasonable purchase price ceiling and hit the 20% mark, then we definitely have a flip candidate worth bidding on. In reality, the Ditmore property came back at 30% and the Meadow property came back at 18%. We track our expenses by these same categories and then do a comparison to see in which categories we need to improve our budgeting skills. In both of these properties, we were able to sell them at a higher price than expected. This really improved the Ditmore margin percentage. The Meadow percentage was lower due to the unexpected furnace replacement and much higher costs in the drywall, baseboards, trim, and doors.

Write the Offer

Disclosure Documents

Once you've done all of your research and chosen the property you want to flip, the next step is the offer. The offer includes a few signatures. The first few documents you sign will likely cover any disclosure agreements with your real estate broker. These documents describe the nature of your relationship with your real estate agent. For example, is she only representing you, or is she also representing the seller, called dual agency? In almost all cases you prefer that your real estate agent only represents you. If she is only representing you, she will put your interests in front of hers. If she is representing both you and the seller, then she is required to put your interest and the seller's interest in front of hers, seeing both sides of the deal, which can be difficult to stay neutral.

Residential Property Disclosure (RPD)

The next document you will sign is the Residential Property Disclosure (RPD) form. This is an important document, whether you are buying a flip property or a turn-key property. This form is the document where the seller must disclose a lot of information about the property. This form will tell you any issues the property has had in the past or has in the present, and it's vital that you review this document before signing the offer.

We discovered the Meadow property was in a flood zone when we reviewed the RPD document during the purchase and understood this might be a risk when trying to sell it. When we completed this document for the sale of the property, we very clearly confirmed that this property was in a flood zone. What we didn't realize was the buyer's agent missed this when going over the documents with the buyer. He didn't realize the property was in a flood zone until after the inspection and appraisal were finished. The mortgage lender actually brought it to the buyer's attention. He initially wanted to cancel the contract, but his real estate agent ended up paying the first-year's premium in order for him to agree to finalize the purchase. Understanding and reviewing these documents are important. You don't want to get two weeks into the process and then discover a detail that was there the entire time. Do not count on your real estate agent to tell you everything. They are almost always working with multiple clients at one time and may easily miss a detail like this. You, as the buyer or seller, need to review the documents yourself before signing any of them, especially the RPD.

Purchase Contract (Offer)

This is where paying all cash for the property really helps your case. When you write the offer paying all cash, you have complete control over the requirements of the offer. Many flippers opt to remove all of the contingencies of the offer. For example, they will not require an inspection for the deal to close. They will not require an appraisal. There is no financing contingency in the offer. Not having an inspection, appraisal, or financing contingency almost guarantees that if the offer is accepted, the deal will close. This gives the seller more confidence in you as a buyer.

On the other hand, if you have 20% down, the bank will require you to purchase an inspection and an appraisal. Most banks are not willing to take a risk that their collateral (the flip property) isn't worth as much as the loan, and therefore require the appraisal. The inspection also avoids them holding a property as collateral that is structurally not sound or in need of significant termite damage repair. Even if you receive a pre-approval letter, this doesn't guarantee that your loan will close, meaning you also need to have a financing contingency. If you can't get a loan for the property, then you won't be able to close the deal.

Because there is more risk for the seller when the offer comes from someone who is financing versus someone who is paying all cash, the all-cash buyer can generally get the property for a discounted price. The discount isn't as great as you would think, however, when there are multiple offers.

In the Meadow flip there were no other offers against ours, with the exception that it was an estate sale. The county had appraised the property at sixty-eight thousand dollars, but our offer was fifty-nine thousand dollars. Because we were the only offer, the real estate agent representing the seller's estate had to go back to the estate judge and ensure the fifty-nine thousand was accepted, which it was. We got a deal because we had the cash to pay with no contingencies.

In two other experiences we were in a multiple offer situation and didn't fare so well. In the first, we were bidding for a tiny seven-hundred square foot home in very poor condition. We offered twenty-three thousand dollars all cash, no contingencies. The other party offered thirty thousand dollars, but they needed financing. The seller went ahead with the thirty thousand offer and it closed. These flippers did an amazing job on this small property and sold it for one-hundred and ten thousand dollars nine months later. If they had had all cash, they could have bid twenty-four thousand instead of thirty thousand and beat us.

In another scenario there was a property with ARV of one-hundred and eighty thousand dollars. We bid ninety thousand dollars and were in first place for a while, but then someone who needed financing came in at one-hundred thousand dollars. The seller went with them. There were five bidders on this property. It's currently being renovated and also looks amazing on the outside.

Evidently, having cash doesn't guarantee that you will win the property, but it does speed up the closing time and generally results in a bigger discount on the property.

Negotiation

Once you've determined the purchase price you will offer to the seller, it turns into a waiting game. Your real estate agent will present your offer to the seller's agent and give reasons for the low-ball offer. It's her job to plead your case to the seller's agent, to explain the justification for the low offer. If there are multiple offers, there won't be much of a negotiation. In the case of multiple offers, the seller's agent must present all of the offers to the seller. They review them together and choose the best one from their perspective, whether that means best price or best deal as in no contingencies.

One point to consider is your real estate agent's time. Real estate agents do not want to insult sellers. When you throw out a number that is too low, your agent should warn you that the price might offend the seller. You are trying to get a good deal on a property, but the seller is also trying to get the maximum value he can. This was likely his home, and he has many memories here. Don't offer so low that the seller refuses to negotiate or to counter back to your original offer. Also, don't throw out so many low offers to sellers that you waste your agent's time. Your agent only gets paid when you close on a property. If you are consistently putting out offers that are unreasonable, your agent may get frustrated with this behavior and end her relationship with you.

Negotiation is most important when only your offer is on the table, competing with no one else's offer. The Ditmore property was our best negotiation. They originally listed the property at eighty thousand dollars. The property was in a nice area, but it was filthy and full of trash. We offered fifty thousand originally. They countered our offer at seventy-five thousand. We countered back at fifty-five thousand, and then we heard crickets. We had made the sellers mad by not countering any higher. We knew, however, that they were delinquent on their property taxes and were about to get foreclosed on by the county. After we didn't hear anything, we went on looking at other properties. We didn't get in a hurry or counter back higher. We moved on. About a month later we noticed they reduced the list price to sixty-five thousand. We offered fifty-eight thousand, and they finally accepted. It was a long negotiation, but patience won out in the end. The pressure they were facing from the impending foreclosure helped our case as well. We ended up getting a good deal on this property, and they didn't have to go through a foreclosure. They actually walked away from the closing with a decent check due to the equity they had in the property. It was a win-win deal for both parties in the end.

Close the Deal

In case you haven't experienced purchasing real estate, this is what to expect. The length of the purchase process can take time and can be stressful as you are wanting to close and move forward. These steps below assume you are not removing any of the standard contingencies in a purchase contract (offer). However, if you are paying all cash, you may skip the inspection, appraisal, and financing steps shown below. We actually did go ahead and get an inspection for the Ditmore property, but we skipped it for the Meadow property.

Request to Remedy (Inspection Window)

Once you have the accepted offer from the seller, you generally have a 10-day window to order the inspection and send the seller the items you want to be repaired or remedied. Most flip properties are going to have items that need to be repaired. Most sellers sell these properties 'as is', meaning they have no intention to make any repairs in order to close on the sale. In this case, the inspection would serve the purpose of proving to the bank that the property is not condemned or has anything too significantly wrong with it. In our case we ordered an inspection for the Ditmore property because we were still relatively new to flipping and wanted to ensure we weren't missing anything significant beyond what we could see. On a side note, the buyer pays for the inspection usually immediately after the inspection is finished. This is where paying all cash can save you a few hundred dollars if you bypass getting an inspection.

Appraisal

Once the inspection is completed and the bank has contingently approved you, the appraisal is then ordered. Again, the buyer is responsible for paying for the appraisal. This is an additional few hundred dollars that could be saved if you're paying all cash. If you are paying all cash, there is no reason to get an appraisal. The only value you care about is the future expected sales value or the ARV.

If financing, the appraisal must come in at or higher than the value of the purchase price. Lenders generally don't accept anything lower. If the appraisal does come in under the purchase price, then the buyers have two options. They can either bring in more money at the closing to cover this difference or they can renegotiate with the seller. Luckily, our appraisals have always come in high enough when selling our flip properties.

Title Search

Once the appraisal comes in as expected there is a title search done to ensure the property is really owned by the seller. The title search will show all of the current owners of that property at that time. The title company will then issue title insurance to the buyer, usually paid for by the seller. This insurance covers the buyer in case anyone would come forward and say they were the legal owners of the property. For example, if the seller and his sister both actually owned the property, then the sister would also need to sign the final documents transferring the ownership to you. This title search confirms who the owners are by a chronological order of the owners of the property from the time the property was built.

This title insurance became valuable on the Meadow property. During the first few months of the project, we noticed every Saturday someone would stick a piece of paper and sticker to the front door. The paper was some type of advertisement for a mortgage. I called the number on the paper to tell them to stop putting these on the front door. They wouldn't stop. They also claimed they had a lien on our property. I tried explaining that we paid all cash, and there should be no liens on the property. After I was unsuccessful, I got in touch with our title company. They had similar struggles to get information, but the attorney was able to find the right person at this reverse mortgage lender. After he provided proof that the lien was paid and demanded they stop harassing us, they finally stopped. This was a long process and had we not purchased the title insurance, that lender might still be harassing the owners of the flip property. Title insurance is a must when purchasing property, even if you are paying all cash.

Final Background Checks & Documents Prepared

At the same time as the title search, the lender is also doing background checks on you to confirm you completed your application accurately. There is a verification of employment to confirm you have had steady income for at least two years. They are repulling your credit report to ensure you have not gone into any additional debt in the last thirty days. Once the lender has all of this completed, the loan documents and title documents are prepared. The closing then generally happens at a title company.

There are closing costs in every real estate transaction. There are exceptions, but almost always, the seller pays the real estate commission for both the seller and the buyer. The seller also generally pays for the title insurance, but this can vary from state to state and even county to county. The buyer pays for the appraisal, lender fees, and some of the title fees. There is a prorated property tax that generally is paid for by the seller and credited to the buyer, since most property taxes are paid in arrears.

Once everyone signs the documents and the keys are handed over to you, you're ready to start the renovation!

7: Execute the Renovation

How to Contribute Best (Labor vs Outsourcing)

Do It Yourself

How much do you know about construction or remodeling? If the answer is nothing, it's okay. You don't need to be an expert on every single piece of the renovation. There is a lot that flippers can do for themselves that aren't too difficult; they just take a little muscle and some persistence. For example, almost anyone can demo. This includes taking off wallpaper, pulling up carpet, potentially tearing out drywall, and removing cabinets and counters. As long as you avoid the plumbing fixtures and the electrical wires, almost anyone should be able to do this piece. In addition, you can pull up all of the staples remaining after the carpets have been pulled up, you can operate a power washer if this is necessary on the exterior, and you can trim trees that need to be groomed. DIY is the least expensive route, but it is also the most time consuming. If you're working full time and don't want to spend your weekends at the property, then you may not want to go this route. As the flip progresses, however, there is work that goes beyond my own skill level. For example, I don't have any interest in learning electric, but luckily, Deb does. She is also a competent plumber, but the Meadow property was in an area that required a licensed plumber in order to get the permit signed off. Therefore, we hired a plumbing company for all of those changes. We do as much of the work ourselves as we can without breaking any county permitting requirements.

While Deb is working on electric, I am either framing in new walls and closets, installing insulation and drywall, or painting. We usually work on the drywall mudding and sanding phase together, as these are both tedious jobs that neither of us like very well. These are all jobs that seem to get better with practice. I felt I improved immensely on my mudding and sanding skills from the Ditmore property to the Meadow property. You may not feel comfortable doing some of these projects, but if you want to learn, it is likely easier than you think. Other projects that aren't too difficult to learn are installing tile, backer board, and laminate floors. We've been able to learn these skills as we've done more flips. In addition, we both have great families, who have helped with many of these projects.

Once we are finished with the paint and electric, we can then install the kitchen cabinets, which we've done ourselves. My dad usually cuts the butcher block counters to ensure they are accurate, and we install the backsplash ourselves.

When it comes to the more technical items, such as a new furnace, hot water heater, or air conditioner, we hire a vendor. We haven't come across this yet, but we would also hire a vendor to replace a roof if it was necessary. There are some projects where it is better and safer to let the professionals handle it.

Hire a Contractor

If you want to outsource the entire project to a contractor, you will need to do a lot of research about the contractor upfront. For example, will he cover all types of work or does he only specialize in a few areas? How much is he going to charge? What happens if there are overages? Does he stick to his estimate or add on additional costs? Will he actually do everything he says he will in the amount of time he quotes?

If you decide to outsource everything, your renovation will go much faster, but you still need to be hands-on. You'll need to project manage the renovation, by getting updates and being onsite frequently to make sure progress is really being made. You can't trust everything your contractor tells you even if they have done a good job in the past. Contractors generally commit to too much work. They want to stay busy in slow periods. They hire their own teams and need to ensure their employees are busy to keep producing enough income to cover the team's wages and overhead costs. If they have more than enough jobs, then they will be less likely to go through a down period. The problem is that they generally can't hit every deadline they commit to. This is why you need to visit the site to confirm what he is telling you is the truth.

Contractors also hire subcontractors, which are usually not employed by the contractor, but hired by the contractor for specific jobs. This may reduce the accountability of the subcontractor if the contractor is not keeping tabs on him. If you're not hands-on and present at the property, you will have to believe everything you are being told, which might not be accurate. Communicate, communicate, communicate. It's very easy to miscommunicate. The more you are in touch and present at the flip property, the less likely communication will be an issue.

You do not need an in-depth knowledge of how to do the work that you want done, but you do need to have some concept of how each item gets done in order to make sure the contractor isn't inflating hours or over-charging you. In my first flip, I hired one contractor to put up vinyl siding and replace all of the windows. His timing was great on the windows. He had them replaced relatively quickly, but then I didn't see him for a while. I called to see what was going on, and he confirmed he had promised another person he would complete her project. He had a small crew, and they were juggling different jobs, just like most contractors. I was firm with him that the siding needed to be completed by a certain point in time, and he committed to that date. He and his team worked twelve-to-fourteen-hour days starting around 6am to avoid the heat, but they were able to complete the work, and the house looked great. You have to stay on top of the contractors, because they can easily get distracted with other jobs even if they've proven they were reliable in the past.

Evidently, having a contractor manage your projects is much faster, especially when you are working full time. You'll be able to complete the renovation quicker and may be able to do multiple flips per year. The downside is that it will cost much more than doing it yourself.

Employ a Team

If you really want to flip properties full time and eventually want to quit your full-time job, you may want to hire a crew. If you hire directly, you have more control of that person's time. He would only be devoted to your properties. The problem, however, is that you need cash to pay someone a full-time or part-time salary, and to find a quality person, you're going to need to pay him what he can get from other construction jobs. You'll need to commit up front to a certain number of hours per week or month. This is almost impossible if you have a full-time job. The amount of commitment and volume of properties you will need to keep this crew busy would also occupy a lot of your time. If you have the cash to keep them paid consistently and the drive to do multiple flips at one time, hiring a team may be the best value for your money. They will be less expensive than contractors, but they may need more managing and coaching as well. Just because you have a team doesn't mean they don't need supervision or management. Everyone needs direction and accountability at times. You'll still need to be present at the flip properties to ensure the work is progressing as expected.

Use Vendors

Vendors are different than contractors. Vendors generally specialize in one or two areas where a contractor can usually offer a wide variety of services because he can hire subcontractors in each of those areas. When choosing vendors, get multiple quotes. If you are just starting out and don't have a relationship with any vendors in town, get a few quotes to ensure you are getting the best deal. We hired a vendor to install a new furnace and used a plumbing company to install the rough-in for both bathrooms at the Meadow property. We received multiple quotes, researched their reviews online, and made a decision based on our impression of the person who came to do the estimate. Both companies provided excellent customer service, were timely, and had reasonable costs.

The more flips you do in the same area, the more likely you are to create relationships with these vendors. Through these relationships, you may be able to get volume discounts or loyalty discounts if you stick with the same vendors on all of the flips. Another opportunity that might come up is these guys generally know people in their field. For example, our plumbers knew independent contractor plumbers. In our case, the plumber vendor actually hired an independent contracting plumber to work one of the days at our flip property. If we had known this independent contractor earlier, we could have likely received a significant price discount by hiring him directly. If we do another property in need of plumbing work, we have the choice of hiring the plumbing company or the independent contractor.

The more flips you complete, the more likely you are to meet new vendors. Use these interactions as data points and opportunities for your next project. Any money you can save here can be spent on more tangible aspects of the renovation.

Seek Other Flippers

Get to know other flippers. Relationships with other flippers can be beneficial in many ways. Deb and I worked with a couple that were also flipping properties. The husband actually decided to start flipping full-time last year after they had successfully completed a couple flips. They invited us to an open house they were having at one of their flip properties. The purpose of the open house was a celebration of the completed project with the vendors and contractors who had helped complete it. I was busy on the day of this open house, but this would have been an excellent opportunity to network.

We learned this flipping couple found their drywall independent contractor on Craigslist. He was reasonably priced and had quality work. They've used him on every property since. We also learned these guys keep security cameras at all of their flip properties. Luckily, they had cameras at one of the properties as someone broke in and tried to steal some of their tools. With the camera capturing this intruder, this couple immediately called the cops, and the thief was arrested. We have learned many tips from these flippers' experiences and have shared our experiences with them. It's great to share best practices.

Maximize the Design

The final look and feel of the flip property will either attract buyers or scare them away. From this perspective, the design of the property can make or break your net profit on the project. It's crucial that you get the design right. It would be a shame if you put all of your money, time, and hard work into a property and then ended up not getting the design right and not being able to sell the property. If you don't have an eye for design, hire someone. You do not need to spend significant funds on a designer, but find someone you know, a relative or friend, who has good taste and see if they will help you for a small fee.

How to Decide What to Update

You'll need to make a decision on what projects you are willing to take on. Do you want to focus on properties that allow for only cosmetic changes? How do you define cosmetic? Some might call new paint and new floors cosmetic. Some may take it a bit further, installing new vanities, toilets, and showers. It doesn't matter how you define it; it matters that you decide what projects you are willing to take on. For example, replacing the hot water tank and the furnace are expensive items. They do not produce an aesthetic improvement to the house since they are generally buried away in a utility room. They do, however, provide some security to the buyer if they have been replaced recently. These are expensive updates, and anytime you can find a property that doesn't need these items to be replaced is a bonus. These are almost a given like you expect safety on a flight, buyers expect the mechanicals of their home to be reliable and working.

The rooms that give the biggest bang for your buck are the kitchen and bathrooms. People spend a lot of time in their kitchens. Almost every family get-together involves food of some sort. If you're having a get-together at home, there will be people cooking in the kitchen. Having a decent sized kitchen is important. Anything you can do to make the space feel bigger is a plus. We removed the wall between the kitchen and dining room in the Meadow flip in order to give the space a bigger feeling. Light colors work well too. We have installed white cabinets in all three of the kitchens we've done. New cabinets and counters make the space feel clean and bright. Storage seems to be in an endless shortage as well. Make sure you add enough cabinets for someone to store all of their pots, pans, dishes, and food. The three kitchens we've done were the shining stars helping to sell our three flip properties.

In addition to the kitchen, bathrooms also sell homes. The latest trend is having a master suite. Many people desire the convenience and privacy of a master suite. Again, in the Meadow flip, we reconfigured the layout to create a master suite with a double vanity. This was a huge selling point. Having a second bathroom also creates convenience for the buyers, even if it isn't a master suite. In the Ditmore property, we were able to add a second bathroom, but because of the layout, we weren't able to make it a master suite.

Color Pallet & Consistency

The property should shine by the end of the renovation. It should radiate neutral colors consistent throughout the property. You may want to add an accent wall here or there, but the overall paint color should lean toward the lighter side and should be consistent throughout the house. By keeping the paint color light and neutral, the space will seem bigger. When you use darker colors, they make the space seem smaller than it really is.

Before purchasing one item, think through how all of the items will look together. For example, if you choose a white kitchen cabinet with butcher block counters, make sure those colors tie into the backsplash and wall color. Bathrooms and kitchens will likely have the most surfaces which need to be coordinated. Think through the entire room before making purchases. We have used the same tile flooring for both bathrooms in the Ditmore and Meadow flips. We stick with a brushed nickel finish for all lights, door knobs, faucets, and cabinet pulls, which gives a modern look.

Similarly, think about the baseboards, trim, interior doors, and flooring. If you decide to only take on a few projects, make sure the rest of the house flows with those updates. For example, sometimes you walk through a house and you can feel a difference in one room to the next, seeing where the original house ends and the addition begins. All of the materials and styles change from the front of the house to the back. In the same sense, when you only renovate certain areas, you may run into this issue, where some rooms are alike and others are not. Whichever projects you decide, make sure there is cohesion throughout the entire house.

The Meadow property appeared to be a hodgepodge of multiple additions with different heights for each of the additions and different trim in each of the rooms. We stripped off all of newer trim and baseboards and left as much of the original baseboards as we could. We then purchased some poplar boards and cut them using a table saw to imitate the angle that the originals were cut at. We were able to put consistent trim and baseboards throughout the entire house. Even though the rooms in the back of the house had much lower ceiling heights, the baseboards and window trims were all consistent from the front of the house to the back. Also, the paint color was the same throughout the entire house as well as the flooring and interior doors. We used white doors throughout. We also used a laminate flooring throughout the entire house with the exception of the two bathrooms. When you remove walls to open up the space, it's vital that you also keep the same flooring throughout. If you were to remove a wall, but still keep two different flooring types in each of the original rooms, the flow would not exist.

Consistency and cohesion allow the house to flow better and makes a great impression on potential buyers.

Layout

The current trend seems to be that buyers want open concept. Open concept is a newer trend, however, and most flip properties you purchase may not have that open feel. It may be required that you remove some walls to create this feel. I have actually torn down a wall in all three of the flips I've done. In the Elm property we removed about six feet of a wall to open up the kitchen to the living room. This made a huge difference when you first walked into the house. In the Ditmore property, we completely reconfigured how this property worked. It had a bad layout when we purchased it due to an addition. We improved the layout by moving the kitchen to a different spot in the house, which helped to open up the house. In the Meadow property, we removed the wall between the kitchen and dining room, opening up this space and letting natural light flow through. Anything you can do to open up the space in the property and configure it to a more functional space will add value to the property that you can recoup in the sales price. As a side note, before you remove any walls make sure they are not load-bearing walls. If the wall is holding up the house and you do not add support, your flip is going to cave in on itself. Most contractors can tell you which walls are load bearing and which are not.

Another trend regarding layout is having a master suite. This wasn't very big in the 1950's and 1960's, so, again, many houses may not have this feature. Master suites are convenient though, and buyers want convenience. In the Meadow property, we were able to take the original bathroom and connect it to the master, creating that master suite. We were then able to add a second bathroom to the home. We wanted to add a master suite to the Ditmore property, but the layout was so strange that it wasn't feasible with our budget. We did create a second bathroom where the kitchen had been originally, giving the property two bathrooms and four bedrooms.

Another vital layout consideration is the design of the kitchen. Buyers want a kitchen they can easily work in. The most common way to create a convenient kitchen is to create a triangle with the refrigerator, stove, and sink. There shouldn't be too much blocking the way of these three areas in the kitchen. This allows for easy access when cooking. If possible, try to design the kitchen with a cook in mind. Make sure it has enough space for multiple people to be in and make sure these three items are easily accessible between one another.

Making the Most with Bargains

A company was closing one of its plants in our area, and we were able to get a bathroom sink, interior paint, and backsplash tile for almost nothing. These were quality items, but because of the company's situation, they were selling them for pennies on the dollar. We are always looking for bargains or clearance items when renovating a property. However, we do not buy cheap quality items. We may get a deal on a bathroom sink, like we did for the Meadow property, but we compensated by buying a fairly expensive double vanity in the master suite bathroom.

As a flipper, you are always analyzing the cost of the items versus the value they will give to the property. No one wants to walk into a house and think 'cheap'. It's not attractive to be in a space where you know the renovator used the cheapest quality items. It's similar to going into a new build, where the builder used "builder-grade" finishes. The house is new and may be grand, but if it has cheap finishes, you'll never want to pay full price for it. Buying a house has almost always signified 'the American dream'. Although that is an outdated phrase, it's true that buying a house becomes personal to the person who is planning to make that house her home. She doesn't want to feel cheap walking through the front door; she wants her home to reflect her own style: clean, modern, and fashionable.

Always be on the lookout for bargain buys, but never use the least quality items available. For example, in the Ditmore and Meadow properties, we used butcher block for the counter tops. We actually saved a lot of money compared to the granite and quartz alternatives, but we also offered a great-looking product. The buyer's real estate agent for the Meadow property said she had counter envy, seeing the walnut butcher block we had installed. She said she had just renovated her own kitchen and used granite, and she was telling us that she liked our counters better. Find the less expensive alternatives, but keep high quality, and you'll be able to sell your flip properties quickly.

Avoid Rework – Do Projects in the Right Order

One important component I didn't know in the first flip was that projects really need to be worked in a certain order. I understood that you most likely wanted to paint before you updated the flooring, but I hadn't considered for example, that I should have changed out the doors before updating the trim around the doors. This is a simple example I learned after completing the first renovation. Each property we complete gives us a better idea of what projects need to be done when.

On the Ditmore flip I was too rushed to install the drywall and start painting instead of waiting for the electric to be finalized. This resulted in us having to cut a square in the drywall around the switch box, and then having to mud, sand, and repaint this area. By the Meadow flip, we did about every project in the right order.

Be a Project Manager

As I mentioned earlier, you need to have a list of all of the projects you plan to take on during this renovation. Deb and I talk through each of the rooms to make sure we are on the same page with the plan. From the outset we agree on a high-level list of changes we plan to make. We visualize the layout changes and ensure that we both understand each other. Every couple of weeks, we revisit that plan to confirm we are still on the same page. For example, in the Meadow property, we removed some closets which had created a small hallway to the master bedroom. In place of those closets, we added a bathroom and removed the hallway. We closed up two doorways, and then, created a new wall and doorway for this new bathroom. Her and I were on the same page and understood how this would look in the end. Her family had helped quite a bit in the beginning weeks of this project. We described this layout change to them, and I had assumed they understood what it was going to look like. It surprised me later, once the walls were started that they hadn't really seen the vision we had. Deb and I had likely spent more time talking about this change than the time we spent to them describing it, but it was surprising. Communication can easily be misunderstood. Make sure you not only describe your vision, but also ask your partner to describe it back to you to ensure she sees it how you see it.

If you're working with a contractor, it's good to stay in communication constantly about the plan. Contractors have multiple projects going on at the same time. They likely will not be as focused as you are on your flip property. An example of a communication issue we had was getting our new furnace installed. We moved the cold air return in the Meadow house to help the flow and also added a new vent to the new bathroom. The house previously had two cold air returns (vents that pull in air rather than push out heat), and we had asked that the furnace vendor remove one of them. They ended up disconnecting the wrong one. It wasn't a big deal because we were able to correct the duct work, but this is an example of how easily a simple miscommunication can end up leading to the wrong outcome.

Next, let's go through the different steps of the renovation.

Demo

Evidently, you want to start with demo. Demo is a dirty process, and best-case scenario this needs to be completed before starting on many of the other projects. We get a lot of family participation during the demo phase. There isn't a lot of skill required for demo, but there is some muscle that's necessary. Understanding which projects are going to be undertaken is crucial during the demo phase. If you don't know what you're going to change in the property, how will you know what areas need to be demolished? We've had some memorable demo moments. In this most recent flip, we removed the wall between the kitchen and dining room. This was a plaster, load bearing wall that had been there since the early 1900's. It didn't come out easily. Deb's sister, niece, and I all took turns throwing the sledge hammer at this wall. We didn't remove the studs due to the load bearing nature, but we did remove all of the plaster and lathe surrounding the studs.

Demo can be argued to be the most fun of the projects. You don't need to be extraordinarily careful about breaking things, because in most cases you are gutting rooms. Do be careful, however, when demoing near plumbing and outlets. No one wants to deal with having to shut off the main water line due to mistaken damage to the pipes. Even though the demo phase might be fun and might be the best work-out, it can also be dissatisfying. You will most likely make the property uglier than when you first purchased it.

The Meadow property didn't seem to be in horrible condition when we purchased it. It was dirty and gross, but given a good cleaning, it was habitable. Once we started knocking down plaster and dropped ceilings, it took on the look of an abandoned property. For a few months we kept doubting ourselves, saying the property was better before we got to it. It's only through this demo phase, however, that improvement and change can take place. Don't let the haggard look of a demoed property bring down your resolve to complete the renovation. Once we were able to break through the demo phase, it progressively looked better and better each day we were there.

Electrical, Plumbing, & Framing

After or during the end of the demo phase, it's time to start working on the electric, plumbing, and framing. Deb does all of the electric updates to the properties. She spends a good amount of time up in the crawl space running new wire and undoing the existing sloppy electric job. In this last property, the property didn't have access to the crawl space above the ceiling. We actually started by cutting a hole in the kitchen ceiling for temporary access and then created a permanent access in one of the bedrooms. This Meadow property was so old that the original roof was made of wood, and the original lights hanging from the ceiling were powered by gas. It's very interesting to see what's unearthed at these older properties.

At the same time as the electric was getting updated, we were working on the framing of the new bathroom and reconstructed a place for the new shower in the existing bathroom. We also changed the layout of the house by closing off three existing doorways and creating new doorways in more appropriate places. We expanded one of the bedroom closets by removing the kitchen pantry and also closed off what was a small bedroom closet and created a bathroom closet. During this phase we also removed the wall between the kitchen and dining room and installed a header. After the new bathrooms were framed in, we called a few plumbing companies to get quotes and to understand the requirements for the rough-in plumbing.

The plumbers got to work, the electric was being replaced, and we started removing wall paper from the front two rooms. Removing that wall paper took quite a few days of labor and a wall paper steamer. We found writing on the walls that indicated the wall paper had been installed in one room in 1962 and the other room in 1933.

The plumbers were able to get the rough-in done in two days. We then needed to prep the bathrooms for their return. We focused on the bathrooms in order to get the plumbers back as quickly as possible. We installed the new drywall, mudded and sanded the drywall, and finished up the painting. We then installed the backer board and tile floors, and purchased the shower walls, vanities, and toilets. The plumbers returned and finished installing all of the fixtures. These two bathrooms were nearly complete.

If you are replacing doors and windows, this is the time to do it. We replaced one exterior door and installed many new interior doors. Install any doors before adding the new trim.

Drywall & Painting

Luckily, lots of family came to help install the drywall for the walls and ceilings. We had gutted many walls and had a lot of drywall that needed to be installed. On the day we installed the ceilings, my brother, sister, and Deb's parents, sister, and niece helped. We had three drills between us and a few ladders. Fortunately, the ceilings were lower in these three back rooms. We had people holding up the drywall with their heads in order for others to drill. We made it fun and completed the three ceilings in one day. The best part of the day might have been when Deb's dad tried to remove a nail from the wall. He brought in the hammer, looking confidently towards this nail. He took a shot at it with the hammer, and instead, created a new hole in the drywall. When he removed the hammer from the hole, that nail was still there. We had to give him a hard time about this.

Mudding and sanding seem to take us a long time. We usually mud twice, assuming our first layer was smooth. Then, we sand. Then, we mud and sand one more time. It usually needs at least three coats of mud, which draws out this process to a few weeks, assuming we are only working weekends. After all of this is completed, we are finally ready to install the trim around the windows and doors, and then paint. For me, the turning point in every flip we've done is the painting. Once the primer and a couple coats of paint are on the walls, the property takes on a whole new personality. It's no longer a neglected, sad house; it's a house that has new life. Painting the ceilings and walls is done in about five days. I generally take some time off work to get through the painting within a week or two. A coat of paint on the trim is usually done within this week as well, but the trim painting seems to continue all the way through to the end of the project as there always appears to be new spots that need to be touched up.

Once the walls and ceilings are painted, we can then install the new overhead lights, the cover plates on the switches and outlets, and the door knobs on the interior doors. Rooms start to look really good during this phase.

Kitchen

After the walls are painted, we are free to start on the kitchen, installing the cabinets. We have already planned the layout and therefore just need to confirm we are still happy with the original layout. Once this plan is finalized, we purchase and install the cabinets. Once cabinets are installed, we are then able to install the flooring or we can install the counters. This is dependent on which material is available first. If flooring is available, we can usually install the flooring to the entire house in four or five working days. Next would be the baseboards. If the counters are ready, we install them, and are then able to install the backsplash and the cabinet pulls.

Exterior

At the same time, we are working on landscape and exterior items on the house. For example, at one flip property, the house had wood siding that needed to be painted. Deb's family came over and helped us. With all of their help, we were able to get two coats on in one day. On the Meadow property, it had decent vinyl siding already, but really needed to be power washed. Deb's dad did that for us in a day.

The good thing about making progress on the renovation is that once some projects are finished, it opens up multiple projects that can then be worked on. Some days you may not feel like doing something inside, and instead you work on the exterior. The flexibility of the work is great for when you want a change. It's important to know what needs to be done before what. This is something that took us a renovation to learn. But, by the third flip we did everything in order, avoiding much of the potential rework that could have arisen. We still had rework though. No project will ever go perfectly, but by following an order, you'll minimize the amount required.

Meet the Neighbors

Neighbors Know the Area

The people who can give you the most insight on a neighborhood are the people who live there. We have been lucky in all three of the flips that the neighbors have turned out to be great people and watched over the property when we weren't there. We never asked them to watch the property, but it's in their best interest to watch over a vacant house in their neighborhood. We try to go to the property at least two to three times a week to ensure no one is camping out inside. We also pack up most of our tools every night and keep them in my truck for safety. If we do leave anything there of value, it is likely hidden somewhere. We try leaving up the curtains or blinds a bit longer after the demo, but at some point, they need to come down. This makes us feel vulnerable because anyone passing by can easily look in the windows. As long at the place looks empty and isn't full of valuable tools, no one seems to be too interested. We have lucked out so far in that we haven't been robbed or vandalized.

We do make it a point to meet the neighbors. It might be the second month before we meet them, but it always happens. They are generally curious about the changes we are making and like to see the progress. We like showing it off too, but when you're at the flip property, you are there to work, not to spend all of your time giving tours. There has to be a balance. One evening after work at the second flip property, the wife neighbor dropped by for a tour. She liked to talk and was there about twenty minutes. Then, the neighbor on the other side decided to drop by for a tour. He also liked to talk and repeat himself. He was there about twenty minutes as well. The wife's husband and daughter came home, and they wanted to see the property. That was another thirty minutes. This was an evening where we had planned to be there for two hours. We lost over an hour giving tours. This wasn't a productive day. Sometimes you need a break, and giving tours can be fun. But, know when it's time to get back to work.

Neighbors can be Watchdogs

I mentioned this earlier, but our neighbors were such watch dogs in the second and third flip properties that Deb had visits with the local police at each property. In the Ditmore flip I had left to pick up some items at Lowes, and the neighbor happened to see movement in the house with no vehicle in the driveway and called the cops. In the Meadow flip the neighbors didn't recognize our vehicles yet and saw what appeared to be an unknown vehicle parked by the house and called the cops. Deb was a little offended this happened to her twice, but it also gave us the reassurance that our neighbors were watching out for us. On one other occasion, a neighbor told us that the previous owner, who was getting ready to be foreclosed on, decided to visit the property when we weren't there. He happened to catch her looking in the windows and demanded that she leave.

Another neighbor of the Meadow property also gave us his opinion on renters. He was adamant that if we decided to rent out this property, he wanted our phone numbers. We learned that the other neighbors referred to this neighbor at the neighborhood mayor. He knew about all of the happenings in the neighborhood and wasn't afraid to speak his mind about how he felt about the other neighbors and how they maintained their properties. This was more insight we had. We hadn't planned to rent out the flip property, and based on conversations with him, it sounds like we made the right choice.

Neighbors Know the History

Lastly, we were able to get insight on the history of the property. One of the other neighbors of the Meadow property actually helped to take care of the man who lived there previously. He mentioned the previous owner hadn't maintained the property for the prior ten years or so. He also told us the previous owner didn't smoke which was a huge surprise to us, considering all of the walls and windows were lined in a dirty yellow layer. On the Ditmore flip, we found out from the neighbors that we had purchased the 'druggie' house and that there were likely over-doses that had happened in the property. All of the surrounding neighbors were excited to get those previous owners out of the neighborhood.

Get to know these neighbors as they can provide insight that might help you picture your future buyer better, and it's a win-win for both parties as a flipped house can increase property values of the entire block.

Quality is Key

Quality is a priority, even higher than profit margin. One test I've given myself is that by the end of the project, no matter which projects were undertaken, is the property a home I would live in? If I can answer 'yes' to this question, then I feel the quality given on the renovation was up to par. So far, I can say that I would have lived in all three flip properties. I actually did live in the first one. Quality is significant, especially as you continue to do flip after flip. Real estate agents will start to know you and your work. Your reputation precedes you. If you do quality work, then real estate agents will recommend your properties to their clients. You know what happens when real estate agents don't like your work. They won't visit, and they won't refer.

On both the second and third flips we completed, we received rave reviews from all of the agents who visited or were involved in the deals. Knowing that we handed over a quality product to the buyers feels very satisfying. Strive for this on every renovation you do. You won't have any regrets, and it will motivate you to do another one.

8: Staying Committed

Power of Focus & Goal-Setting

Flipping a property is a monster under-taking especially if you plan to do most of the work yourself, and especially if the renovation is extensive. By listing all of the changes you want to make on the flip property, you'll have a high-level plan. But, looking at the list and trying to accomplish too much at the same time or in the same day is overwhelming. Each day you work at the property, you need to have a couple goals, or even just one goal. During our commute over to the property, Deb and I would discuss what our goals were for that day. By having just one or two goals for the day, you don't have to think about everything else that needs to be done; you only have to work on those small projects. For example, we both hate mudding and sanding. We each took a bathroom, and the goal was to get each bathroom sanded and another layer of mud on before we left that day. Another day we went over with the goal to tile both bathroom floors. We did this on an evening after work. I thought this job might take us two hours, but it ended up taking us four hours. We didn't leave until 9:30pm. That would have been fine in most cases, but when tiling a floor there are many pieces of tile that need to be cut, and the tile saw is very loud. We had it set up on the back deck, where I'm sure all of the neighbors were getting annoyed. We try to respect the neighbor's time and generally don't run loud tools after 7pm or before 9am on the weekends. But, in this case, we wanted to finish these two floors, so we worked later than normal with at outdoor tool. None of the neighbors said anything to us. We tried not to make this a habit, and they didn't seem too bothered by us working later once or twice throughout the renovation.

Having a goal each day allows you to focus in on one small project of the overall renovation. Focus is the key to achieving any goal. Focus on one goal each day and you'll not only make a lot of progress, but also will feel a sense of satisfaction at the end of the day when you finish that goal. Flipping a property is a marathon. You can't go at it all at once. If you start working on multiple projects within the property, it will take you longer to finish each of them. The longer you work with no significant accomplishments, the less motivated you will be. It's important to set yourself up for success. Projects need to be broken down and focused on one at a time. When you have small wins along the way, you will be more likely to keep going and stay motivated.

Dave Ramsey emphasizes the power of focus in his baby steps. If you want to become financially independent, you can't pay on consumer debt while simultaneously investing in your 401k. His baby steps focus on one step at a time. First, pay off your consumer debt, then after that is paid, save an emergency fund. Once you have established an emergency fund, then start contributing to your 401k. Just like his baby steps, in order to successfully flip a property, you need to break it down into projects. Focus on each project one at a time. Don't try to go back and forth between projects. It will slow you down, and you won't accomplish as much. Have your goal at the beginning of each day and work until that goal is accomplished. This is how you'll see the most results.

Self-Discipline

In addition to staying focused, self-discipline is a must. Flipping is not easy. It takes a toll on you physically and emotionally. It's a long process and can be stressful. If you do not commit to spending time each week at the flip property, you will be in for a very long project. Depending on the scope of work the property needs and how much of the work you do yourself, you're likely looking at four-hundred to one thousand hours of your time. If this was your full-time job, this might be simple. But, if this is your part-time job, and you're already spending forty to fifty hours a week at that, it leaves less time for you and your family and hobbies.

Deb's hours and my hours totaled around eight-hundred on the Ditmore flip and one thousand on the Meadow flip. These were roughly split down the middle between the two of us. We generally spent about ten to sixteen hours each per week at the flip properties. This usually included both Saturday and Sunday. There were a few weekends we took off, but then made them up throughout the week. Completing a flip is similar to investing. If you only invest a few dollars here and there, then you won't end up with much. If you only spend a few hours here and there at the flip, you're not going to finish in a reasonable time. To complete the project, you'll need to be disciplined in spending time at the property just as to retire comfortably, you'll need to invest consistently and considerably throughout your lifetime.

Persistence

Persistence pays off. It's this intangible value that some people have and others don't. In order to be successful flipping, you'll need to be persistent. You'll need to fight through the difficult times. There will be stressful and frustrating moments at the flip property, just like in most full-time jobs. You'll need to fight through these to come out ahead on the other side. The easiest way to fail at flipping is quitting. No one wants a partially demoed, partially renovated house.

To build your pipeline of properties, you'll also need persistence. The first few times you reach out to real estate agents, advertise, or talk to homeowners, it most likely won't go well. Unless you have experience counseling, coaching, and persuading people, it's going to take a few conversations to understand the right responses and to remove emotion completely. It's very easy to let our emotions interfere, but flipping is a business. You have to see it this way and not take things personally.

80/20 Principle

I just finished reading Richard Koch's "The 80/20 Principle". Basically, this principle says that 20% of our activities or resources produce 80% of our profits or income. You can exchange the words I've used. For example, you could also say that 20% of your friends give you 80% of your enjoyment, or in a business setting, 20% of your products give you 80% of your revenue. The percentage isn't always 80/20. It can be 95/5 or 70/30, but the point is that a few of the total activities can produce many of the results. When flipping, once you figure out what activities create 80% of the leads for deals, or which improvements in the properties create 80% of the buyer demand, you'll know what to focus on.

For example, find out which method of searching for properties works most effectively for you. When you discover which method of finding properties is best for you, it will also most likely be the method that requires the least amount of energy on your part. Maybe networking with real estate agents works best for you and drives 75% of your flip property leads, and the sum of all of the other methods you try only provides 25% of your leads. You would likely stop working the other methods and focus your attention on talking to real estate agents.

We all have a limited amount of time. It's best to find what works for us and be as efficient as possible, expending the least amount of energy and getting the best results.

9: Sell the Property

The time has finally come. You have almost completed the renovation. For me this is the most exciting time of the project. It's time to test whether all of those updates you made were worth it or not. You find out if you picked the right property, if you spent the right amount of money, and if you are going to make a profit. In both the Ditmore and Meadow flips, the real estate market was hot, and they sold very quickly at above the asking prices. That's the best feeling to be under contract with a buyer. However, just because you get under contract with a buyer doesn't mean the deal will close. In the Elm property, I was in contract with a buyer, and the deal eventually fell apart. After the inspection, she wanted about fifteen items changed. Some of these were petty, and I didn't have a good feeling about it. I only agreed to remedy five of the items she had requested. She didn't like this and canceled the contract. This initial contract wasn't meant to be, because a week later I was under contract with a new buyer at a higher price. If a deal falls through on you, don't sulk about it; it wasn't meant to happen. Get the property back on the market and see if there is a better offer out there. In my experience I did end up with more cash from the second contract.

Once you've agreed on terms and sales price with the buyer, don't assume the deal is done. There are almost always a few contingencies that need to be fulfilled first. Just like when you purchased the property, you had the option to give yourself some contingencies in case you wanted to back out of the deal. The first contingency is usually the inspection. It's standard that buyers ask for a ten-day window after the offer is accepted to get the inspection completed and the request for remedy, which lists all of the changes the buyer is asking for, submitted. For example, a good inspector will check the house from top to bottom. In the Meadow flip, the only item the buyer wanted corrected was some termite evidence, therefore we hired a termite company to kill any living termites. In the past we have had items such as gutters needing to be cleaned, adding a GFCI outlet to the kitchen, and a new man door for the garage. Based on the inspection report, buyers have the right to ask for any change they want. If they really want the property, however, they will generally keep their requests to a minimum. On the other hand, you, as the seller, have the right to say yes or to say no to those changes. Depending on your response, the deal might move forward or it might not.

The next contingency that might hurt the deal is the appraisal. Assuming the buyer is financing the flip property, the lender will require that the appraisal is at least as high as the purchase price. In the Ditmore flip, we had multiple offers which were driving up the price. Our real estate agent kept warning us that the appraisal was never going to come in at this high value. She advised that if it came in lower, we should be prepared to accept the appraisal value as the new sales price. Astonishingly, the appraisal came in above the sales price and the deal went through.

Another item that can spoil a deal is if the buyers can't get financing to purchase the property. In almost all cases buyers will attach a preapproval letter to their offer, indicating how much they have been preapproved for by their lender. When a lender preapproves a buyer, they are simply doing a high-level check on those buyers. When it comes to actually lending money to the buyers, there is a much deeper check done. For example, did the buyers not tell the entire truth when they told their lender they had the 20% down in the bank? Did they go out and purchase a new vehicle since they had been preapproved? There are many reasons a lender can decide later that these buyers are no longer qualified.

There are many reasons deals go south. Remember this as you are reviewing the initial offers. When you have that check in hand at the closing, then you can really celebrate that the deal is closed.

To Stage or Not to Stage

All three of our flips were listed on the market without any staging. You've seen on HGTV that they almost always stage their properties, but staging can cost a lot of money and time. We choose lower-valued properties to flip, and we don't have the extra time or money to spend on staging the properties. If you renovated the property by improving the layout and the flow of the property, buyers shouldn't need to see furniture in the property for them to visualize what the space will look like.

I don't see us staging any flip properties in the future. We have been successful without this step. If you do want to give staging a try, think about your strategy. Will you hire this out entirely? If not, are you confident enough in your design choices to find furniture that enhances the overall look of the house? Will you rent the furniture or will you purchase the furniture? If you purchase the furniture, will you try to sell the property including the furniture or will you store the furniture in order to use it at the next flip property? You'll need to be able to answer all of these questions if you decide to go down the route of staging. Answering these questions allows you to estimate the number of hours and total cost of staging. Make sure you add this to your budget and timeline.

What to Include When Selling

Deb and I disagree on the appliances that should be sold with the property. She doesn't think we need to purchase a refrigerator for example. However, we have been able to get great deals when buying the package of appliances, including the stove, microwave, dish washer, and refrigerator. As long as we keep getting good deals on the package, it makes sense for us to install all four appliances for the buyer. Buyers who are looking for turnkey properties want convenience. They want a home they can move right into with minimal hassle. This is why they are looking at renovated homes and newer homes. Not offering a refrigerator adds another item for the buyers to have to deal with. So far, we have always installed all four appliances together and have been successful. By buying these together, we are not only getting a deal on the price, we are also ensuring the appliances match. We do not install a washer and dryer though. This is one inconvenience buyers have to purchase separately when buying one of our flip properties.

Another debate we have are the blinds. In the Ditmore flip, we left the windows bare. In the Meadow flip, I was able to convince Deb we needed them. This was due to safety and privacy concerns. The flip property does look a bit more finished with blinds as well. Because I had lived in the Elm flip, the buyers received all of the appliances, the washer and dryer, and blinds and curtains.

Curb Appeal

When putting the property on the market, a first impression of the place will win or lose potential buyers. Curb appeal is important. We replaced the front and back steps and deck on the Meadow flip because the existing steps were rotting. The look of the new wood not only brightened up the curb appeal, but also had a solid feel when walking over them.

Other major items included brand new siding on the Elm property. Siding is expensive and most likely does not give you the best return. But, in this case it was worth it. It really improved the look of the exterior. The Ditmore property already had wood siding that was salvageable. We found replacement wood siding for the pieces that had rotted, and then painted the entire house. The paint made the property really stand out and made it look fresh. The third property already had siding. Deb's dad power washed the siding for us. He gave the house a whole new life by removing all of the soot and grime that had accumulated over the years.

We also replaced the address numbers and mailboxes on all three properties, giving them an updated and cohesive look. All three yards hadn't been maintained for years prior to us purchasing them. We dug up a countless number of uncontrolled trees and bushes. When cutting out bushes, make sure you either dig up or cut out the stumps. No one wants to see a yard full of stumps, and especially no one wants to mow around or over them. Simple landscaping, such as planting flowers, adding mulch, and giving some order to the exterior goes a long way to improving the appearance of a property.

Curb appeal is the first thing a potential buyer will see when they scroll through the Realtor or Zillow apps. That one picture needs to draw them in and gain enough interest for them to click on your property's profile. Curb appeal is also the first thing your potential buyer will see when driving down the street looking at the 'For Sale' signs. Although I didn't spend much time going through the exterior projects, they can have the most impact with regards to how many eye balls see the online profile and how many visitors actually sign up for a showing of the property. The more eye balls, the better chance of finding that right buyer.

How to Determine the Sales Price

How do you decide what to price your flip property? Being the owner, you will likely be biased toward a higher price. This is where it helps to have a third-party, neutral real estate agent on your side. That agent can search what comparable homes have sold for in the last ninety days. She can do all of the research for you and present you a CMA (comparative market analysis). This will show you the area in which the comparable properties are located, how big they are compared to yours, and how much they have sold for. Having all of this information helps you determine the most appropriate sales price.

We had an agent represent us on the first two properties. In talking to her and seeing the market myself, we were able to come to an agreement quickly on the list price. On the third property, Deb and I needed to come up with the list price on our own since I played the role of our real estate agent. After I researched the recent sales prices of comparable properties, we looked at the price per square foot that the other properties sold for and used this value to come up with our list price. We ended up using a lower, more conservative price to gain some interest. We were hoping for a multiple offer situation. But, instead, we ended up selling higher than our list price with just one single buyer's offer. He was purposefully offering a higher price to avoid us moving into a multiple offer situation. We went back and forth a few times with him, but were able to agree on a price.

Make sure you know your comparable properties and understand the differences between the properties. For example, one of the comparable properties might be the exact same house, same square footage, and same yard, but the comparable is in a nicer part of town than yours. Every difference needs to be considered when determining the list price. We have found in our experience, it's almost always better to list the property at a slightly lower value than you believe it's worth. The lower price gains more interest, and you almost always end up at a higher agreed price in the end. You don't want to price your property too high and then find out that no one is interested in it. By pricing it too high, you will gain higher days on the market which gives buyers a higher incentive of negotiating down on your list price.

You should already have a few comparable properties in mind based on when you purchased the flip property. Depending on how long it takes to complete the project, you may be able to use those original comps or you may need to look for new ones.

How to Market the Flip Property

In order to market the first two properties, we used the same real estate agent. Going through an agent gets the property added to the MLS (multiple listing service). The MLS is a database of all of the properties for sale in a specific area. Only real estate agents and some third parties have access to this database. I, as the real estate agent on the third flip, listed our property on the MLS. This process gets your property a lot of eye balls. You want as many people as possible to know that your property is for sale. In addition to listing the property for sale on the MLS, we shared that we were hosting an open house through the MLS. We also put out signs in front of the property, told our families and friends, and posted it on Facebook. Having an open house brings in other buyers and real estate agents who are curious about the property. We invited all of our neighbors to this open house as well. I did make a mistake though. We listed the property on Thursday and advertised the Sunday open house on that Thursday. By Friday we were already under contract. Therefore, we didn't even need the open house. We ended up having a small open house for friends, family, and neighbors, which turned out great. The reason I had posted everything on Thursday was to give everyone a few days to see it before the actual open house on Sunday, but now I know that properties can move much quicker than in three days. This quick offer and acceptance were not a bad thing though. It was awesome to be under contract roughly twenty-four hours after having listed the flip property. When listing your flip property, think of ways to get the word out. You want everyone you know near that area to see it and share it with their friends. The more people that know about it, the higher the probability of finding your buyer sooner.

10: Summary of Flipping Rules

Flipping is not an easy endeavor. It's difficult in many ways, but it is also one of the most satisfying and rewarding hustles I've ever done (and I've tried quite a few). The tangible results that come from flipping real estate give me true satisfaction. Cleaning up the neighborhood and helping a buyer find a home is a great experience. The work and project management requirements are difficult though as well as the timing of the cash flow. You will work many months without seeing a dime. Once you complete the project and find a buyer, however, you will receive a nice big check. If you can handle the labor and contractors, have a basic understanding of design, and can commit to a project, this is the part-time hustle for you.

I hope the guidance in this book is helpful to your successful part-time hustle of flipping. I've summarized the top guidance I follow when flipping real estate. Follow these rules and your chances of losing money drop dramatically.

Don't Over-Pay for the Property

Don't let yourself get emotionally attached.

Flipping is a business. Treat it that way in your heart. Don't get emotionally attached to any piece of property and pay too much. This is the quickest way to lose at real estate.

In real estate the money is always made at the buy.

The price you pay to purchase the flip property makes or breaks your profit potential on the project. Understand the significance of your purchase price and don't wreck it.

Be able to walk away from any deal. Patience is key.

There is a property on almost every block of the street. If the one you're bidding on now doesn't work out, it's not the end of the world. Walk away and find a better deal.

(ARV – ARV*6% Real Estate Commissions – $4,000 – Purchase Price Ceiling– Renovation Cost) / ARV => 20%

This formula works. Determine the ARV and the renovation budget, and make sure you offer under this calculated purchase price ceiling. Reducing the 20% to anything lower doesn't make sense. You can invest in mutual funds and make 10%-12% on average without any flipping hassle. Why would you mess with a flip property if you've only got 13% return planned?

Unexpected issues are bound to come up even if you do have a contingency. Don't exceed the price you come up with in this formula as the reality is that you may end up with less return.

Plan, Plan, Plan

Most of the content of this book focused on the planning of the flip versus the execution of the flip. This wasn't by accident. Planning is important in every aspect of life, but it is especially important when jumping into the world of flipping. There are some great quotes that highlight the importance of planning and preparation. "By failing to prepare, you are preparing to fail" was said by Benjamin Franklin, and "good fortune is what happens when opportunity meets with planning" by Thomas Edison.

Purchase Price Ceiling

Know your purchase price ceiling ahead of time. If you go to an auction or are part of a bidding war, things can heat up very quickly. Make sure you know your ceiling before you enter. And, obey that ceiling price. You've determined what this purchase price ceiling is before you entered the offer. Don't let the thought of 'winning' the competition by being the highest bidder throw you off course. If you end up the 'winner' by paying fifteen thousand dollars over your ceiling, you haven't won anything. You've signed up for a lower profit with the same amount of work to get there. If you don't end up with the property, you haven't lost anything. Go and find another property.

Budget

Evidently, to determine the purchase price ceiling, you're going to need a budget. List all of the projects you'd like to improve in the property, and then determine roughly how much each one will cost. Add in a contingency for any projects you decide to do later or any items you may have overlooked. No one gets a budget exactly right, but having a budget gives you an idea of what projects you're going to work on, how much materials will cost, and how much labor will cost. By having this idea, you'll know upfront how much money you need in the bank to carry out this renovation.

Timeline

In addition to the budget, the timeline is important as well. Understanding all of the projects you will undertake allows you to come up with a rough timeline of the entire renovation. This timeline gives you an indication of when you can get your money back and start the next flip. Don't be overly optimistic on the timeline. You'll find once you start these projects that many take longer than expected.

After we finished the Ditmore flip in October 2018, I was ready to conquer another flip. We purchased the Meadow property two months after we sold the Ditmore property. I became overly ambitious, writing out a timeline that showed we were going to finish three flips in that following year. That did not happen by a long shot. We ended up just selling the Meadow property by November of that year with no progress on any other properties. It's good to be ambitious, but be realistic too. If your full-time job is anything like mine, it takes up a lot of time. There are only so many additional hours in the day, and weekends are only two days long. Be realistic when determining your timeline.

Complete the Flip

The last rule, which I'm sure you know by now, is complete all of the renovations you start. If you try to sell a property that is only partially renovated, you will lose money. When I'm a buyer and I see a half-demoed property for sale, I get excited, because I know I'm going to get a good deal on the property. The sellers have actually done me a favor because I have less demo to do myself.

Avoid selling a half-renovated and half-demoed property if you can. I know flipping a house is a lot of work, and you may not understand everything you're getting into when you start flipping, but don't give up prematurely. Fight through the frustration. You've done your budget and timeline, so you have enough cash to get through this. Keep your eyes on the end-goal and keep looking forward. You might be at the point where the house looks worse than when you purchased it. This is a really difficult phase to go through. Even on the third flip, I still had my doubts while in this phase. But, stick to it and work through it. The finish line awaits. The property will look amazing on the other side.

Conclusion

I hope you gained some insight from this book and are ready to tackle a flip property. Flipping real estate is an awesome part-time hustle. It's challenging, satisfying, and stimulating. It can bring out the best in people and the worst in people. The challenge is mental, from negotiating the right price, understanding the right projects to pursue, and budgeting appropriately. The challenge can also be physical, depending on how much of the labor you do yourself. You make these decisions. You are your own boss.

I wish you well on your flipping journey!

www.ingramcontent.com/pod-product-compliance
Lightning Source LLC
Chambersburg PA
CBHW050002230526
45465CB00003BB/1217